99

EASY TO MAKE WINE

WITH ADDITIONAL RECIPES FOR COCKTAILS, CIDER, BEER, FRUIT SYRUPS AND HERB TEAS

EASY TO MAKE WINE

WITH ADDITIONAL RECIPES FOR COCKTAILS, CIDER, BEER, FRUIT SYRUPS AND HERB TEAS

BY

MRS. GENNERY-TAYLOR

Originally Published in England as Easymade
Wine and Country Drinks

GRAMERCY PUBLISHING COMPANY · NEW YORK

This edition published by Gramercy Publishing Company,
a division of Crown Publishers, Inc.,
by arrangement with Elliot Right Way Books
d   e   f   g   h

Manufactured in the United States of America

PREFACE

THIS book is intended for the ordinary housewife or perhaps her husband.

I hope it will be helpful to those who wish to make a few bottles for home consumption or for giving to friends.

I have tried to show that good wine can be made in small quantities and with simple equipment. I therefore hope my book will encourage some of you to start this fascinating hobby.

I should also like to thank those friends who have so kindly let me use their own special recipes.

I affectionately dedicate this book to my parents and to Charles for suggesting it, I say, 'thank you'.

CONTENTS

PART I: GENERAL INSTRUCTIONS

PART II: WINES

CONTENTS

PART III: WINE RECIPES

PART IV: OTHER DRINKS

PART V: CHILDREN'S DRINKS, TEAS AND COFFEE

TABLE OF LIQUID CONVERSIONS

BRITISH	AMERICAN
1¾ pints	4¼ cups or 1 quart 2 ounces
¾ pint (generous)	2 cups (generous) or 1 pint (generous)
3-4 ounces	½ cup (scant) or ¼ pint (scant)

EASY TO MAKE WINE

WITH ADDITIONAL RECIPES FOR COCKTAILS, CIDER, BEER, FRUIT SYRUPS AND HERB TEAS

GENERAL INSTRUCTIONS

——

HINTS ON WINEMAKING

Soon after I married I decided to make some wine. I had never made any and had no idea how to begin. I remembered that my grandmother used to make excellent wine but I was a child then—too young to learn.

I was lucky, however, in having a good friend who could make wine. To her it was an inherited accomplishment, handed down from one generation to another, as necessary to housekeeping as cooking.

She gave me a recipe for rhubarb wine and as it was springtime there was plenty of rhubarb about. I followed her directions carefully and found everything absurdly simple. But still I didn't believe that this fruit juice could become wine.

I filled the wine bottles and placed them in a cool dark cupboard. Never was wine watched so carefully. I inspected and tasted it nearly every day. Hapless visitors were forced to try it, but my husband revolted—he would rather wait till it was ready to drink.

Somehow I managed to save two bottles for six months and found, secretly to my surprise, that it had turned into a very pleasant wine. This greatly encouraged me, and I began to make different kinds and have done so ever since.

Of course I had some failures, sometimes I was careless and the winefly got in and turned the wine sour.

Other times I left too much airspace in the bottles and the wine turned sharp. But gradually I learned to be careful and watch for these things.

Although we are not constantly drinking wine, I rarely seem to keep a bottle for much more than a year to mature properly. I firmly hide several bottles but there is always that special occasion which seems to demand a bottle of wine. So my stock dwindles.

I love trying new recipes or inventing my own.

I FIND THAT THE MAIN VIRTUE NEEDED FOR WINEMAKING IS PATIENCE.

ECONOMY

One thing that consoles me when I see my wine disappearing so quickly is that it is much cheaper than shop wine.

I believe the cheapest shop wine is about 12s. a bottle, whereas home-made wine can cost less than a tenth of this. In many cases, where wild fruits or flowers are gathered, sugar is the only ingredient to be bought. So this wine costs not more than 9d. a bottle.

One can also be extravagant in using it for cooking. Home-made wines can often take the place of white wine or sherry. There is no need to use the wine sparingly when one knows there are some more bottles in the cellar.

UTENSILS AND CONTAINERS

Please do not be put off making wine by the thought of the expensive equipment to be bought. Most of us have a large saucepan or preserving pan which will do to boil those ingredients which need boiling.

METAL CONTAINERS MAY BE USED AT THIS STAGE, *BUT MUST NEVER BE USED TO HOLD FERMENTING WINE.*

Next you need a large bowl, a big earthenware mixing bowl will do. A plastic bucket makes an excellent container for your mix, because it is light, easily cleaned and easy to cover.

Bottles are the next item. Keep all your old lemonade or wine bottles, those with corks are best. Most types hold just over a pint of wine.

The only other things you will need are a wooden spoon for stirring and a piece of butter muslin or fine net for straining. So the following àrticles are all you really need:

>1 large saucepan or preserving pan.
>1 large earthenware bowl or plastic bucket.
>Some old lemonadade or wine bottles.
>A wooden spoon.
>A piece of butter muslin.
>A plastic funnel.

If you wish to make sufficient wine to be able to enjoy it freely and to build up a mature stock for special occasions, it is advisable to make not less than a gallon at a time: $1\frac{1}{2}$ or 2 gals. can be made with very little extra effort and therefore a 2 gal. or $2\frac{1}{4}$ gal. bucket is worth having.

Earthenware crocks, formerly used, are becoming scarce; they are comparatively expensive, heavy and harder to handle. Wooden casks are favoured by advanced amateur winemakers fortunate enough to possess them, but they require careful use and are certainly not essential, as good wine can be made with the simple equipment specified in this book.

Other very useful containers are gallon jars which save space, as one will hold six bottles of wine.

Glass jars, also corks to fit them and small plastic fermentation locks, can be obtained from Messrs. Boots Chemists. They are inexpensive and preferable to earthenware jars because it is possible to see exactly how fermentation is progressing. A fermentation lock is a simple device which permits gas to escape through water but prevents air entering.

FORMING A MOULD

In the first stage of some wines, the fruit has to be left in the bowl till a mould has formed on the top. This should be removed in one piece if possible. Try to avoid little pieces breaking off into the wine.

Sloe wine can be left for months, till a really thick mould has formed. Country people say of sloe wine, " The better the mould, the better the wine."

Wine often looks rather unpleasant at this stage, especially the flower wines. It doesn't seem possible that this horrible concoction can turn into a clear sparkling wine. I can assure you it can, so don't be discouraged.

THE WINEFLY

Wines fermenting in bowls or other containers must always be covered closely with a clean cloth to prevent the winefly from entering. This tiny fly appears almost from nowhere it seems, at the mere whiff of fermenting wine. if it does get into the wine in large numbers it will soon turn it sour, so be most careful to keep the bowl completely covered.

FERMENTATION

Fermentation begins in the large container, after sugar

(and yeast where required) has been added; it requires some warmth and an air space below the covering material, therefore at this stage keep the container in a place where the temperature is 60°–65° Fahrenheit; e.g. alongside an all night burning stove or radiator. If the container is nearly full some liquid will froth over.

You can tell if wine is fermenting by listening for you will hear a faint hissing noise. In a clear glass bottle if you hold it to the light you will see masses of tiny bubbles rising.

Another test is to put a little sugar in the bottle. If the wine has finished working or fermenting then nothing will happen. If it is still fermenting the sugar will make it fizz, often right over the top of the bottle. This shows that the yeast in the wine still needs feeding, so add a little sugar or sugar candy.

When you are sure the wine has finished fermenting, push the corks in tightly and put the bottles away to mature for as long as possible. It will keep for years.

CLEARING THE WINE

Wines should clear themselves in time, but to make sure, a little isinglass may be added while the wine is still fermenting.

Dissolve $\frac{1}{4}$ oz. of isinglass in a cup of water and pour gently into a gallon of wine.

This is not essential, and I have never used it, because even a stubborn wine clears in its own time. However, if you wish to hasten the process, then isinglass is the answer.

STRAINING THE WINE

I find butter muslin the best material for straining wines. Straining is most easily done by laying the muslin across a plastic flour sifter (borrowed from kitchen); lodging the sifter across a plastic bucket and pouring the wine through.

On no account use a metal strainer, this could react to the acid in the wine and probably turn it black.

FILLING THE BOTTLES

The strained wine can be quickly bottled without waste by using a plastic funnel. Fill the bottles almost to the top but leave some air space below the cork and cork loosely. As fermentation will be continuing, the corks will frequently blow out and will have to be replaced promptly; consequently daily inspection will be necessary. Time and trouble may be saved by tying the corks in loosely in the following way.

Take a piece of string about 15 inches long; double it and knot it to form a loop about $1\frac{1}{2}$ inches long; tie the free ends of the string round the neck of the bottle making this knot opposite the loop. Then thread one of the free ends through the loop which draw across the top of the cork and tie with other free end in such a way as to allow the bottom of the cork to rise under pressure of fermentation to say within $\frac{1}{4}$ inch of the top of the bottle. The gas will then escape round the edges of the cork, but while the pressure of fermentation continues no more air will get in to spoil the wine.

The odd half bottle of liquid which is usually left over can be used for filling the bottles. You will find sometimes, that after the wine has been fermenting, the level in the bottles has sunk a little. Fill the bottles up from the spare bottle. Of course this small amount will not keep long if left in a large bottle as the airspace will turn it sour. I find it better to keep this spare wine in a small bottle, such as a medicine bottle. When a bottle of wine is opened for use, it should not be kept more than a few weeks as it will go sour.

In the recipes that follow, the periods specified for transfer to bottles, after sugar (and yeast where recommended) has been added, vary from 3 to 14 days; these are minimum periods and more time can be allowed safely and profitably, provided that the original container is covered effectively.

FEEDING THE WINE

Some wines improve if fed with sugar candy. This is a very hard sugar, strung together in lumps. I remember it used to fascinate me as a child. I thought it much nicer than ordinary sweets. It only costs a few pence more than granulated sugar and a pound lasts a long time.

The candy is added in small pieces, two or three weeks after the wine is bottled. I find it helps also to clear the wine. The more candy added to the wine the more the alcoholic content increases, until it reaches the point when the alcohol destroys the yeast.

Wheat wine especially needs feeding with candy and as a result it becomes very strong, in comparison with other wines. It is often compared to whisky, having rather the same flavour and colour, but of course not the same alcholic content.

If when tasting a wine it seems rather sour or sharp, some sugar candy added to the bottle will usually improve matters. Ordinary sugar may be used but it is not so effective as the candy. This can be obtained at most big grocers; if you cannot buy it, use one dessertspoon

of demerara sugar to each bottle.   W. R. Loftus, Ltd.,
supply sugar candy at their shop, or by post.

RACKING

When fermentation is apparently finished and the wine
has cleared, it is time to put the wine into its final bottles
and cork firmly.   It is a simple operation to siphon off
the clear wine with a thin plastic tube without disturbing
the sediment or lees, which will be visible at the bottom
of the bottles or glass jars.   This process is known as
racking.

Some wines take much longer than others to clear, but it
is pointless to rack them before hand and it is here that
patience is essential.

STORING WINE

Ideally, wine should be stored in a cool, dark place pre-
ferably on a stone floor, at a temperature of 55 degrees.
But it survives quite well under less perfect conditions.
So don't worry if you live in a flat with no nice cool cellar
or pantry. Find a cupboard that is not too near a fireplace,
and use that.

IT IS BEST TO INSPECT THE BOTTLES
FAIRLY OFTEN AS THE CORKS DO SOME-
TIMES POP OUT, THEN THE LITTLE WINEFLY
POPS IN AND TURNS THE WINE SOUR.

It has been suggested that the wine bottles should be
turned on their sides as professional wine-makers do. This
might however, be difficult in the home where storage
space is often limited. I think if the bottles are filled and
the corks pushed in tightly this should prevent the corks
from drying out and shrinking and so letting in the air.
As a precaution, the tops of the corks may be waxed.

YEASTS

The yeasts I have included in the recipes are Bakers' yeast. Dried yeasts which are easily obtainable nowadays are equally effective. (It is only for beer that Brewers' yeast is advised.) For those who can afford it, however, special selected wine yeasts in dry or liquid form can be obtained. It is claimed that the use of these bring out the maximum bouquet and alcoholic qualities of the wine as well as making the clarifying easier. They are obtainable from the famous old firm LOFTUS Ltd., 1–3, Charlotte St., London, W.1.

This firm specialise in the supply of home made wine equipment and a visit to their premises or a request for their catalogue is an education.

BASIC AMOUNTS AND METHODS

You may find you wish to make wine from some fruit, flower or vegetable not mentioned in this book. The general rule then is:

For flower and fruit wines:

Pour the boiling water over the fruit or flowers and leave to stand for about a week, then strain and add the sugar and yeast.

For root wines:

The ingredients are usually boiled. Then strained over the sugar, and the yeast added when the wine is lukewarm. The proportions are roughly:

3 or 4 lb. of fruit
3 or 3½ lb. of sugar
1 gallon of water.

These vary with different wines and very often other ingredients are added to provide flavour.

If it is a wine that simmers, use about fifty per cent more water to allow for evaporation.

Halving the ingredients to make less wine will not affect its strength.

You will need to experiment a little, but if you follow these main rules you can't go far wrong.

PART II

WINES

WINES AS REMEDIES

YEARS ago many people depended almost entirely on home-made remedies for their ailments. Quite a number of country people today still believe in them implicitly. Wines are quite important in this role and are a very pleasant way of taking medicine. I am sure if doctors' medicines were so delicious, the Health Service would collapse entirely!

Here are some wines which are, so I am told, safe and certain cures. Anyway a glass of wine at any time is a great morale lifter and may help one to forget one's aches and pains. I must however warn those who suffer from rheumatism, they should never touch rhubarb wine.

Cowslip wine will cure jaundice.
Dandelion is good for indigestion and kidney trouble.
Sloe wine is effective for diarrhoea.
Elderberry taken hot on a cold morning will ward off colds.
Raspberry wine is invaluable for sore throats.
Blackcurrant wine when mulled is excellent for colds and bronchitis.
Barley wine is good for kidney trouble.
And rhubarb wine is bad for rheumatism.

19

CHRISTMAS DRINKS

At Christmas the drinks seem to disappear like magic. What with parties, odd callers and extra drinks for the family one needs to spend a fortune to keep up with the demand. Unless of course one has home-made wine to fall back on.

But I admit, to offer a visitor a glass of home-made wine at this festive season may seem rather tame, so I dress up my drinks a little. I have found that with a little experimenting I can make quite a good wine cocktail with my own wine. I will write out one or two to give you an example, but it only needs a little mixing and tasting to improvise a drink with what you have at hand.

LUCKY DIP

The first one I call "Lucky Dip".
½ bottle of rhubarb wine.
½ bottle of marrow wine.
1 wineglass of ginger wine.
1 wineglass of whisky.
1 wineglass of rum.
1 tumbler of carrot wine.
1 tumbler of ginger beer.

Just mix them all together, it sounds a strange mixture but tastes good.

"GUESS WHAT"

½ bottle blackberry wine.
½ bottle rhubarb wine.
Wineglass ginger wine.
Wineglass port wine.

20

½ wineglass whisky.

Mix together and you have the answer!

ORANGE COCKTAIL

1 bottle orange wine.

1 wineglass whisky.

Dash of rum.

OTHER HINTS

If you prefer brandy or gin as the spirit content just experiment a little using these, of course you can be more extravagant with the spirits if you wish, but as a general party drink I find those I have mentioned quite adequate.

If you have a favourite punch recipe, which needs a bottle of sherry or other wine, substitute a bottle of home-made wine or use half and half.

I had a bottle of beetroot wine which was not really old enough to drink, but I wanted a red wine, so I poured a glass of port into the decanter and poured the beet wine on to it. The flavour was improved and several people praised the wine.

My marrow wine although quite strong already, I thought could do with a fillip for the party season. So to one bottle I added a glass of whisky and to another a glass of rum and corked them down till required. One visitor after having two glasses of the rum marrow wine said he felt quite tipsy on going out into the air and was jolly all the way home.

So, if like me, you have to economise at times, remember these tips. It requires little spirits or port and it is so much nicer to be able to serve out drinks with a liberal hand, instead of with one eye on the bottle all the time.

21

A CALENDAR FOR WINEMAKING

It is often hard, especially if one happens to live in a town, to remember when is the time for making various wines.   People who live in the country are more fortunate as they can see when the different flowers and fruits are ready.

This calendar will act as a reminder.   Town folk on a fine day can pack their lunch and sally forth to the country to search for the fruits and flowers of the fields and hedgerows.   The country folk can just step outside their doors any day and help themselves, to the wild flowers and fruits at least, not I hope, to the farmer's wheat or sugar beet.

There are wines to make in every month, plenty to keep the most industrious person busy, but I don't think many people could find the storage space for so many different varieties.   However if you can only try a few there should be enough to ensure a very merry Christmas.

The dried fruit wines can of course be made all the year round.   I have only included them in the winter months when there are not so many varieties of fruit and vegetables to be found.

The weather influences the season of the flowers and fruits, in a cold year they may be late and in a warm year a bit earlier, but it doesn't vary more than a week or so. Some things such as grapes and pears can be bought at any time in the shops, but the out-of-season varieties are too expensive for wine.

WINE CALENDAR

January
Potato, Wheat, Barley, Raisin, Ginger, Fig, Dried Apricot, Dried Peach, Orange.

WINES

February
Potato, Wheat, Barley, Raisin, Lemon, Fig, Parsnip,
Dried Apricot, Dried Peach, Ginger.

March
Coltsfoot, Lemon, Tea, Parsnip, Turnip, Potato, Carrot,
Barley, Dried Fruits.

April
Dandelion, Parsnip, Turnip, Carrot, Tea, Ginger,
Dried Fruits.

May
Dandelion, Rhubarb, Marigold, Cowslip, Elderflower,
Gooseberry.

June
Strawberry, Marigold, Dandelion, Elderflower,
Rhubarb, Gooseberry, Plum.

July
Blackcurrant, Redcurrant, Raspberry, Cherry (Clove
Carnation), Plum, Bullace.

August
Peach, Apricot, Loganberry, Pear, Plum, Grape,
Bullace, Carnation, Marigold, Mulberry, Damson.

September
Grape, Pear, Plum, Damson, Blackberry, Carrot, Beetroot, Marrow, Quince, Mulberry, Elderberry.

October
Apple, Blackberry, Hip, Haw, Grape, Sloe, Sugar Beet,
Marrow, Carrot, Elderberry, Turnip, Quince, Beetroot.

23

November

Apple, Sugar Beet, Marrow, Mangel, Potato, Orange, Wheat, Barley, Carrot, Lemon, Tea.

December

Orange, Lemon, Rice, Apple, Tea, Wheat, Barley, Raisin, Dried Apricot, Dried Peach, Fig, Ginger.

An Idea

For final bottling, one can syphon off (using a piece of thin plastic tube) the wine from one bottle to the final bottle. This helps to avoid disturbing the sediment.

PART III

WINE RECIPES

APPLE WINE

> 3½ lb. cooking apples.
> 3 lb. granulated sugar.
> 1½ gallons cold water.
> 2 lemons.
> 1 orange.

WASH the apples and cut out any bad places. Do not peel or core but cut the apples into pieces and put them through the mincer. Now put the minced apples in a large bowl and pour 1½ gallons of cold water over them.

Cover the bowl and leave for a week, but stir well every day using a wooden spoon. After the week strain the liquid off through muslin into another bowl or jug.

Add the 3 lb. of granulated sugar and the juice and grated rind of the two lemons and one orange. Stir well till the sugar has dissolved, then cover the bowl and leave for twenty-four hours. It is then ready to strain and bottle.

This is a delicious fruit drink when it is first made— my children simply love it—and it is quite safe for them as it doesn't start to turn into a wine for a week or so. If you can leave if for four months you will find it has turned into a very clear pleasant tasting wine.

Cork the bottles rather loosely at first and gradually push them in as the wine stops working.

FRESH APRICOT WINE

4 lb. fresh apricots
(weight after stoning).
3½ lb. loaf sugar.
1 gallon boiling water.
¼ oz. yeast.

Stone the apricots, cut them into small pieces and place these in a large bowl.

Pour over them a gallon of boiling water, and stir well. When cool add yeast. Stir every day for five days.

Strain through muslin into another bowl or jug. Add the 3½ lb. sugar and stir daily for three days. Don't forget to keep the bowl covered except when stirring.

The wine is now ready to bottle. Cork loosely at first, and have a look each twenty-four hours to see that the corks stay in. When you are sure that fermentation has finished, you can push the corks in tight. Store in a cool dark place and leave for at least six months before drinking.

Make sure the bottles are kept filled for you may lose some of the wine by the fermentation causing it to fizz over the top. Keep a spare bottle to fill these.

Taste the wine now and again and if you think it needs some more sugar it won't hurt to add a little.

DRIED APRICOT WINE

> 2 lb. dried apricots.
> 3½ lb. granulated sugar.
> 1 gallon cold water.
> ½ oz. yeast.

Wash the 2 lb. of dried apricots and place in a large bowl. Pour over them a gallon of cold water and leave to soak for twelve hours.

Pour the apricots and water into a large preserving pan or saucepan and bring to the boil. Simmer till tender.

Strain off the liquid carefully through muslin into a bowl containing the 3½ lb. of granulated sugar. Stir this well and leave till lukewarm, then stir in the ½ oz. yeast.

Stir daily for four days, don't forget to keep the bowl covered when not stirring. It is now ready for bottling. You may need to strain it again before bottling.

Add a little sugar candy to each bottle after three or four weeks. Ready to drink in nine months.

The apricots left after straining off the liquid will make jam if some sugar is added, about 4 to 5 lb. Make it in the usual way for dried apricot jam, adding a little water of course.

BARLEY WINE

1½ lb. barley
1 lemon.
1 orange.
3 lb. granulated
   sugar.
½ teaspoon ground
   ginger.
½ oz. yeast.
1½ gallons water.

Put the barley into a large saucepan or preserving pan, and pour on 1½ gallons of cold water. Place over heat and bring to the boil. Simmer for about half an hour, then strain through muslin into a large bowl.

Add the sliced lemon and orange, 3 lb. granulated sugar and ½ teaspoon ground ginger. Stir well till the sugar has dissolved.

When the liquid is still lukewarm, stir in the ½ oz. yeast. Cover the bowl and leave for fourteen days, then strain and bottle.

This wine will need feeding occasionally with sugar candy; put a little in each bottle every three weeks or so.

You can drink the wine after six months but it improves with age. Keep it a year or so and it will become very strong, a wine really worth drinking.

BEETROOT WINE

3 lb. beetroot.

3 lb. granulated sugar.

6 cloves.

$\frac{1}{2}$ oz. yeast.

$1\frac{1}{2}$ gallons water.

Wash the beetroot well, but do not peel. Cut it into thin slices and put into a saucepan or preserving pan with the $1\frac{1}{2}$ gallons of water. Bring it to the boil and simmer till the beetroot is tender but not mashy.

Strain off the liquid, and throw away the beetroot, or remove the skin and cover with pepper, salt and vinegar, and eat it. Put the liquid back into the saucepan, add 3 lb. sugar and six cloves and heat just enough to melt the sugar, stir well all the time.

Let the liquid cool till it is lukewarm then pour it into a bowl. Add the yeast spread on a piece of toast.* Cover the bowl carefully and leave for three days, then remove the toast and strain the wine and bottle.

Cork loosely at first; you may find it needs a little sugar candy added after four or five weeks. Just drop a little piece into each bottle.

It should be ready to drink in six months, but the longer you keep it the better it will be.

---

* The reason the yeast is put on toast is to help to keep it from the bottom of the wine. If bread were used it would break up too easily.

BLACKBERRY WINE (BRAMBLE)

3 lb. blackberries.
3 lb. granulated sugar.
1 gallon boiling water.

Gather the fruit when ripe on a dry sunny day. Wash the berries well to remove any maggots which so often get into blackberries.

Place the blackberries in a large bowl and pour over a gallon of boiling water. Stir well, then cover the bowl and leave for ten days.

Strain the liquid off carefully through muslin making sure that no pips or pulp get through. Add the 3 lb. granulated sugar and stir well. Cover the bowl and leave for another three days but stir daily.

Cork loosely at first, and see that the corks do not pop out and leave the wine exposed to the air for any length of time.

This wine should be ready to drink in six months. It is a lovely dark red wine and rather sweet. If you can add a glass of port or ruby wine to the bottle just before drinking, you will find it hard to tell the difference between this and the shop wine.

BLACKCURRANT WINE

> 4 lb. blackcurrants.
> 4 lb. granulated sugar.
> 1 gallon cold water.

Strip the blackcurrants from the stalks and wash them carefully so as not to lose too much of the juice.

Put them in a large bowl and crush them well using a wooden spoon. Pour on a gallon of cold water and stir thoroughly.

Cover the bowl and leave for ten days, but no longer. Then strain and add the 4 lb. of granulated sugar. Stir daily for three days, then bottle.

It should be ready to drink in six months.

ANOTHER METHOD

Some people prefer to make this wine with boiling water. Use the same ingredients and quantities.

Wash the fruit and put it into a large bowl but do not crush it. Pour on a gallon of boiling water.

Cover the bowl and stand for ten days, then strain and add 4 lb. of granulated sugar. Stir till it has dissolved, then cover the bowl and leave for another three days, stirring daily. Then bottle.

Ready in six months.

BULLACE PLUM WINE

4 lb. bullaces.
4 lb. granulated sugar.
1 gallon boiling water.

Bullaces are best when picked after a frost. Wash the fruit and place it in a large bowl.

Pour over the fruit a gallon of boiling water and stir well, with a wooden spoon.

Cover the bowl and leave for about three weeks or until a thick mould has formed.

Remove the mould carefully, in one piece if possible, and strain the liquid off into another bowl or jug. Add 4 lb. of granulated sugar and stir well until the sugar has melted. Cover the bowl again and leave for three days.

The wine is then ready to bottle, cork loosely at first and store in a cool dark place.

Try to leave this wine at least a year before drinking, as it needs longer to mature than some wines.

Taste it after a few months and add a little sugar candy if you think it needs it. This is a very good wine if left to mature for the full time.

CARROT WINE

4 lb. carrots.
3½ lb. granulated sugar.
½ oz. hops.
1 oz. yeast.
1 gallon water.

Scrub the carrots well and cut them into pieces. Put them in a large preserving pan or saucepan with a gallon of cold water. Boil till the carrots are tender, then strain off the liquid into a large bowl. Throw out the carrots, then pour the liquid back into the pan and add 3½ lb. of granulated sugar and ½ oz. of hops. Stir well and just bring to the boil.

Strain into a large bowl through muslin to remove the hops, and leave till lukewarm. Spread the ounce of yeast on a slice of toast and float it on the liquid.

Cover the bowl and leave it for a week. Remove the slice of toast and strain again if necessary. The wine is now ready to bottle. Cork loosely at first.

This may need feeding with sugar candy at intervals of two or three weeks. It will be drinkable in six months, but keep it longer if you can.

CHERRY WINE

5 lb. ripe black cherries.
$3\frac{1}{2}$ lb. granulated sugar.
1 gallon water.
$\frac{1}{4}$ oz. yeast.

Remove the stalks from the cherries and wash the fruit. Place the cherries in a large saucepan or preserving pan and crush them with a wooden spoon.

Pour on a gallon of cold water and bring them to the boil. Simmer gently till the cherries are tender then remove from the heat and strain the liquid off through muslin into a large bowl. When you have strained off all the liquid, tip the cherries themselves into the muslin, and squeeze gently to extract any remaining juice.

Add the $3\frac{1}{2}$ lb. of granulated sugar and the yeast, stir well. Then cover the bowl and leave for three days, stirring daily. The wine is then ready to bottle. Cork loosely at first and add some more wine if any ferments over the top of the bottles. Push the corks in tight when you are sure that fermentation has finished.

You can drink it in six months' time, but keep it longer if you can.

CLOVE CARNATION WINE

> 2 quarts clove
>   carnations.
> 3½ lb. loaf sugar.
> ¼ oz. yeast.
> 1 gallon boiling
>   water.

Pick the carnations, the clove scented kind, on a sunny day. Use only the heads of the flowers, and wash them well to remove any insects. Measure them in a quart jug and you need two jugs full.

Put the carnation heads into a large bowl, and pour over them a gallon of boiling water. Stir well.

Cover the bowl and leave for ten days, but stir daily. Strain off the liquid into another bowl or jug and add the 3½ lb. of loaf sugar and ¼ oz. yeast and stir well.

Cover the bowl again and leave for another five days. After this time stir the wine well and strain again if necessary, then pour it into the bottles.

Cork loosely at first, and keep the bottles filled if they should ferment over the top of the bottle. Keep this wine at least nine months before drinking.

COLTSFOOT WINE

2 quarts of coltsfoot
    flowers.
1 gallon of boiling water.
½ lb. raisins.
1 lemon.
¼ oz. yeast.
3 lb. granulated sugar.

Pick the flowers on a sunny day and measure the quarts while fresh. Shake them well to remove any insects.

Put them in a large bowl and pour on a gallon of boiling water.

Stir well, then cover the bowl and leave for four days.

Now strain the liquid off into a large saucepan or preserving pan. Add the lemon cut into thin slices and the raisins. Just bring it to the boil.

Pour it all into a large bowl and leave till lukewarm. Then stir in the ¼ oz. of yeast and 3 lb. sugar.

Cover the bowl but stir daily for three days. Strain and bottle, leaving the bottles loosely corked at first. Some of the liquid may ferment over the tops of the bottles, fill these with some reserve liquid as necessary.

Ready to drink in six months, but it will improve if you can keep it longer.

COWSLIP WINE

2 quarts cowslip flower.
3 lb. granulated sugar.
½ oz. yeast.
1 lemon.
1 gallon water (boiling).

Pick the flowers on a dry day, only the heads are used. Pick the heads of the flowers off, and measure them into a quart jug, don't press them down. When you have measured two jugs full, wash the flowers well and place in a large bowl.

Pour over them a gallon of boiling water, stir well, then cover the bowl and leave for ten days only.

Now strain the liquid off into another bowl or jug and stir in 3 lb. granulated sugar, add the lemon sliced thinly.

Spread the ½ oz. yeast on a slice of toast and float on top of the liquid. Cover the bowl and leave for three days.

Remove the toast and it is now ready to strain and bottle. You may find that it needs a little sugar candy added after a few weeks; drop a little into each bottle.

This can be drunk at once, but will improve with keeping.

DAMSON WINE. FIRST METHOD

3 lb. ripe damsons.
3 lb. granulated sugar.
1 gallon boiling water.

Choose ripe damsons, wash them and place in a large bowl. Pour over a gallon of boiling water and stir with a wooden spoon. Now cover the bowl and leave till a thick mould has formed on top. This may take weeks, but it doesn't matter as long as you keep the bowl covered. The flavour of the wine will be better if there is a good thick mould.

When you are satisfied that the mould is thick enough, remove it carefully, in one piece if possible. Strain the liquid off into another bowl and add 3 lb. of granulated sugar, stir well with a wooden spoon till the sugar has dissolved.

Cover the bowl and leave for three days. Stir daily. It is now ready to bottle.

Store it in a cool dark place and have a look every few days to see that the corks are still in. You can drink it in six months, but it will improve in flavour if you can keep it longer.

DAMSON WINE. SECOND METHOD

```
3 lb. ripe damsons.
3 lb. granulated sugar.
1 gallon cold water.
```

Pick or buy the damsons as ripe as possible and wash them well. Put the 3 lb. damsons in a large saucepan or preserving pan, and pour on a gallon of cold water.

Bring to the boil and simmer till the damsons are tender but not mashy. Strain off the liquid through muslin into a bowl. The remaining damsons could be used as stewed fruit or for making jam.

Add 3 lb. of granulated sugar to the liquid in the bowl and stir well with a wooden spoon till the sugar has dissolved.

Cover the bowl and leave for three days, but stir daily. It is then ready to bottle. It should be ready to drink in six months, but keep it longer if possible.

If you wish the wine to age quicker, you may add a very little yeast, about a ¼ oz. Stir this in after the sugar has dissolved, when the liquid is lukewarm. This wine may need some sugar candy added after a month or so. You will be able to drink it in six months or perhaps before that. But of course the longer you keep it the better it will be.

DANDELION WINE

2 quarts dandelion flowers.
3 lb. granulated sugar.
½ oz. yeast.
1 lemon.
1 orange.
1 gallon boiling water.

Pick the dandelions on a fine day when the flowers are open. Pick the heads off and measure two quart jugs full.

Wash the flowers very well to remove any insects and put them in a large bowl. Slice the lemon and orange thinly and add to the flowerheads.

Pour over them a gallon of boiling water, and stir well. Cover the bowl and leave for ten days but not longer.

Now strain the liquid off into another bowl and stir in 3 lb. of granulated sugar, spread the ½ oz. of yeast on a slice of toast and float on top. Cover the bowl and leave for another three days.

Remove the toast and strain again, then bottle. Cork loosely at first. You can add a little sugar candy after a few weeks if it seems necessary.

This wine is very nice when new, but of course will improve with age.

ELDERBERRY WINE. FIRST METHOD

5 lb. elderberries.
3 lb. granulated sugar.
½ oz. yeast.
6 cloves.
½ oz. well bruised
    root ginger.
1 gallon cold water.

Gather 5 lb. of elderberries, there are always plenty in the hedgerows. Strip the berries from the stalks; this is easiest to do with a fork; slide it down the stems and push the berries off.

Wash the fruit well, and put it in a preserving pan with a gallon of cold water. Boil till the fruit is tender, then strain off the liquid into a bowl.

Add 3 lb. granulated sugar, 6 cloves, ½ oz. well bruised root ginger and stir well. When the liquid is lukewarm stir in ½ oz. yeast.

Cover the bowl and leave for ten days, then strain and bottle.

You may need to add some sugar or sugar candy after a few weeks, put a little in each bottle but look out, it might fizz out of the bottle.

This wine is very good for colds, especially when taken hot.

It is ready in six months, but better if left longer.

ELDERBERRY WINE. SECOND METHOD

```
4 lb. elderberries.
3 lb. granulated sugar.
3 cloves.
½ lb. raisins.
½ oz. well bruised root ginger.
½ oz. yeast.
1 gallon boiling water.
```

Pick and wash 4 lb. of elderberries. Strip them from the stalks and place in a large bowl. Cut up the raisins and add them to the elderberries, pour over a gallon of boiling water and stir well. Cover the bowl and leave for two weeks.

Now strain off the liquid into a saucepan and add three cloves and ½ oz. well bruised ginger. Just bring it to the boil, and then pour it over the 3 lb. of granulated sugar in a large bowl. Stir well.

When the liquid is lukewarm stir in ½ oz. yeast then cover the bowl and leave it for three days.

The wine is then ready to strain and bottle. It will need feeding at intervals of about three weeks with sugar or sugar candy. Cork loosely at first and see that the corks don't pop out.

Ready to drink in six months but it is much better if kept over a year.

ELDERFLOWER WINE

1 gallon elderflowers.
3 lb. granulated sugar.
1 lemon.
1 orange.
1 ounce of yeast.
1 gallon boiling water.

After you have cut off the stalks measure a gallon of elderflowers. Wash the flowers to remove insects, then put them in a large bowl with the juice and grated rind of the lemon and orange.

Now pour over a gallon of boiling water and stir well with a wooden spoon. Cover the bowl and leave it for four days. Then strain the liquid off into a saucepan and just bring it to the boil. Put 3 lb. of granulated sugar in a large bowl and pour the boiling liquid over; stir well till the sugar has dissolved. When the liquid is lukewarm stir in an ounce of yeast.

Cover the bowl well and leave for another six days, stirring daily. After this time strain again if necessary and bottle, but remember to cork loosely at first. It will need feeding with sugar or sugar candy in a week or so, and probably at intervals of two or three weeks.

Ready to drink in six months.

FIG WINE

2 lb. dried figs.
3 lb. brown sugar.
½ lb. large raisins.
1 lemon.
1 orange.
½ oz. root ginger.
1 oz. yeast.
1 gallon boiling water.

Cut the figs into small pieces and place in a large bowl, with the 3 lb. brown sugar. Chop the raisins and add to the figs. Add the grated rind of the lemon and orange and the juice, but no pith or pips. Bruise the root ginger and add to the other ingredients. Then pour on a gallon of boiling water and stir well with a wooden spoon.

When the mixture is lukewarm stir in the 1 oz. of yeast. Cover the bowl and leave for twelve days, but stir daily.

After twelve days it is ready to strain and bottle. Cork very loosely at first as it will ferment quite a lot. You will probably have to top up the bottles after a while, as some of the wine will ferment over the top. Add a little sugar candy in two or three weeks, and at intervals if necessary.

It is ready to drink in six months but will improve with age.

GINGER WINE

2½ oz. root ginger.
3½ lb. granulated sugar.
2 tablespoons of honey.
Juice of three lemons.
2 gallons of water.

Bruise the root ginger well and put it in a saucepan with three pints of water from the two gallons. Bring to the boil and simmer for half an hour. Into a large jug or bowl put 3½ lb. of granulated sugar, the juice of three lemons and two tablespoons of honey. Pour the ginger and water on to this and stir well. Boil the remainder of the two gallons of water and add to the other ingredients, stir it all well, then leave for twenty-four hours.

After twenty-four hours it is ready to strain and bottle. You can drink it at once, but it will keep for a few weeks if you keep the bottles corked.

I don't waste the root ginger; I put it back into the saucepan with ½ lb. of sugar and a pint of water and boil till the liquid is reduced to a syrup. This is useful either to add to hot drinks, or to use as flavouring in puddings or cakes.

GOOSEBERRY WINE. FIRST METHOD

3 lb. ripe gooseberries.
4 lb. granulated sugar.
1 gallon boiling water.

Wash the gooseberries and put them in a large bowl. Mash them with a wooden spoon, then pour on a gallon of boiling water.   Stir well then cover the bowl and stand for ten days.

After ten days, strain off the liquid into another bowl or jug, and add the 4 lb. of granulated sugar.   Stir till the sugar has dissolved then cover the bowl and leave it for four days.   Stir well every day.

After four days it is ready to bottle.   Remember to cork loosely till you are sure that fermentation has finished.   That is when there is no hissing noise when you put an ear to the bottle, or when the wine looks clear and still, with hardly any bubbles rising.

Push the corks in tight then and see that they stop in. Keep in a cool dark place for at least six months before drinking, and longer if you can.

GOOSEBERRY WINE. SECOND METHOD

```
6 lb. ripe gooseberries.
3 lb. granulated sugar.
½ lb. raisins.
½ oz. yeast.
1 gallon boiling water.
```

Wash the gooseberries and mash or cut them up into a large bowl. Cut the raisins and add to the gooseberries. Add the 3 lb. of granulated sugar and pour over a gallon of boiling water, stir well.

When the mixture is lukewarm, spread ½ oz. yeast on a piece of toast and float on top. Leave for ten days stirring carefully every day.

After ten days remove the piece of toast and strain off the liquid and bottle. Cork loosely at first. Have a spare bottle handy to top up if the wine ferments over the top. Add a piece of sugar candy to each bottle after two or three weeks.

The wine should be ready to drink in six months but keep it longer if possible!

GRAPE WINE

3½ lb. green grapes.
1 lb. black grapes.
4½ lb. loaf sugar.
1 gallon boiling water.

Wash the grapes and put them into a large bowl. Crush them with your hands or a wooden spoon so as not to break the pips. Pour over them a gallon of boiling water and stir well. Cover the bowl and leave it for ten days.

After ten days strain off the liquid into another bowl or jug, and add the 4½ lb. of loaf sugar, stir well. Cover the bowl and leave for another fourteen days, stirring well every day. It is then ready to bottle.

See that the corks don't pop out, and when you are sure it has finished fermenting, that is when there is no sizzling noise when you put your ear to the bottle, push the corks in tight. Leave it for at least six months and much longer if you can, as grape wine improves with age. Inspect it occasionally and add a little sugar if you think it needs it, it shouldn't, but it depends largely on the ripeness of the grapes.

48

UNRIPE-GRAPE WINE

3 lb. unripe grapes.
1 lb. raisins.
2 lb. granulated sugar.
1 lb. demerara sugar.
1 gallon boiling water.

I expect many of you who have grape vines find that in bad summers the grapes will not ripen. There is no need to waste them, they make a really nice wine, I always use mine this way.

Crush the grapes with the hands or very carefully with a wooden spoon so as not to break the pips. Put them in a large bowl, add the pound of raisins cut in halves. Pour on a gallon of boiling water and stir well.

Cover the bowl and leave it for two weeks. Then strain off the liquid into another bowl and add the 2 lb. of granulated sugar and 1 lb. of demerara sugar. Stir well till the sugar has dissolved then cover the bowl and leave for three days, but stir daily.

It is now ready to bottle, cork loosely at first. Taste it after a few weeks and if it seems a little sour add some sugar or sugar candy.

This wine will take nine months at least to mature but try to leave it longer.

GREENGAGE WINE

> $3\frac{1}{2}$ lb. over-ripe greengages
> 3 lb. granulated sugar.
> 1 gallon boiling water.

Wash the greengages and put them in a large bowl. It does not matter if some are a bit squashy, they need to be over-ripe to make good wine.

Pour a gallon of boiling water over the greengages and stir them well, then cover the bowl and leave them for fourteen days.

After this time strain off the liquid into another bowl or jug and add the 3 lb. of granulated sugar, stir well till the sugar has dissolved then cover the bowl and leave for three days.

It is then ready to bottle. Cork the bottles loosely at first, and watch to see that the corks don't pop out. Push them in gradually as the fermentation slows down, and cork tightly when you are sure it has finished.

The wine is ready to drink in six months, but like most wines it improves with keeping.

HAW WINE

6 lb. haws.
3 lb. granulated sugar.
1 gallon boiling water.

Pick six pounds of haws, this will not be difficult as there are plenty about in the autumn. Choose ripe ones.

Wash the haws well and cut off the stalks. Put them in a large bowl and pour over a gallon of boiling water, stir them well and try to mash them a little with a wooden spoon. Then cover the bowl and leave for ten days stirring daily.

Now strain the liquid into another bowl and add the 3 lb. of granulated sugar. Stir till this has dissolved then cover the bowl and leave for another four days, but stir daily.

The wine is then ready to bottle. Cork it loosely at first, and gradually push the corks in tighter as the fermentation slows down. Keep it in a cool dark place and taste after a few weeks. Add a little sugar or sugar candy if it tastes a little sour, but it shouldn't need any more.

You can drink it after six months, but keep it longer if possible.

HIP WINE

> $3\frac{1}{2}$ lb. rose hips.
> $3\frac{1}{2}$ lb. granulated sugar.
> 1 gallon boiling water.

This is a really economical wine as the only ingredient to be bought is the sugar. There are always plenty of hips in the hedgerows; they also contain a large amount of vitamin C, which I should think would be retained in the wine.

Wash the rose hips and cut them in half, put them in a large bowl and pour on a gallon of boiling water. Stir them well with a wooden spoon, then cover the bowl and leave them for two weeks.

After two weeks strain off the liquid into another bowl or jug, and add the $3\frac{1}{2}$ lb. of sugar. Stir till it has dissolved, then cover the bowl and leave for five days, stirring daily.

The wine is then ready to bottle. Cork it loosely at first and store in a cool dark place. Push the corks in tight when the wine has finished fermenting. The wine should be ready to drink in six months, but keep it longer if you can.

LEMON WINE

6 lemons.
1 gallon cold water.
3 lb. granulated sugar.
½ lb. raisins.

Wash the lemons, and peel off the yellow rind very thinly so as not to get any pith left on it. Put the rind into a large saucepan or preserving pan with a gallon of cold water, bring it to the boil and simmer for twenty minutes.

Squeeze the juice from the lemons into another bowl containing the 3 lb. of sugar and ½ lb. of raisins. Strain the water off the lemon peel on to the sugar and raisins, and stir well with a wooden spoon till the sugar has dissolved.

Cover the bowl and leave it to stand for seven days, but stir daily. Then strain it through a piece of muslin and bottle.

Cork it loosely till fermentation has finished. After about a month you may need to add some sugar candy; drop a piece in each bottle.

It will be ready to drink in about **six** months but try and keep it longer.

LOGANBERRY WINE

3½ lb. loganberries.
3½ lb. granulated
  sugar.
1 gallon boiling
  water.

Pick the loganberries and wash them well, but do it carefully so as not to lose too much of the juice. Put them in a large bowl and pour on a gallon of boiling water, stir well and mash the berries with a wooden spoon. Cover the bowl and leave it for ten days.

After ten days strain it into another bowl or jug and add the 3½ lb. of granulated sugar. Stir till the sugar has dissolved then cover the bowl and stand for three days, but stir daily.

Now it can be bottled, cork loosely at first and see that the corks stay in, as sometimes the fermenting wine will gradually push them out, and if it is not noticed the wine may turn vinegary.

It should be ready to drink in six months, but if you want a really good wine leave it at least a year. You can if you wish add a little sugar candy after three or four weeks.

MANGEL OR MANGOLD WINE

4 lb. mangels.
3 lb. demerara sugar.
1 orange.
½ oz. yeast.
1½ gallons cold water.

This is the humble mangel wurzel or mangold. Anyone living in the country should be able to obtain some easily enough. Wait till the mangels have had a frost on them as they will make a better wine.

Wash the mangels well but do not peel them. Slice them thinly into a large saucepan or preserving pan, with 1½ gallons of cold water, or as much water as you can get in. If the pan is not big enough to hold 1½ gallons add some later as the water evaporates.

Bring to the boil, and simmer till the mangels are tender. Strain the liquid off and throw out the mangels. Put the liquid back into the pan with a sliced orange and 3 lb. of demerara sugar, just bring it to the boil, then take off the heat and strain into a bowl.

When the liquid is lukewarm stir in ½ oz. of yeast. Cover the bowl and stand for three days, then bottle. Add a little sugar candy after six weeks. It is ready to drink in six months but of course it will be much better later.

MARIGOLD WINE

4 quarts marigold flowers.
1 lemon.
1 orange.
3 lb. granulated sugar.
$\frac{1}{4}$ oz. yeast.
1 gallon boiling water.

Pick the flowers on a sunny day and wash them well to remove any insects. Place them in a large bowl. Grate the rind of the orange and lemon and squeeze out the juice; add this to the marigold flowers.

Pour on a gallon of boiling water and stir well. Cover the bowl and leave to stand for four days. Then strain off the liquid into a saucepan and just bring it to the boil. Put the 3 lb. of granulated sugar into a large bowl and pour the liquid over this. Stir well till the sugar has dissolved, then leave it to become lukewarm.

When the liquid is lukewarm, stir in the $\frac{1}{4}$ oz. of yeast. Cover the bowl and leave for three days but stir daily. It is now ready to bottle. Cork loosely at first, and fill up the bottles if any of the wine should ooze out of the top.

It will be ready to drink in six months.

MARROW WINE

1 ripe marrow.
1 lb. demerara sugar to each
2 lb. of marrow.
Juice of $\frac{1}{2}$ a lemon to each
2 lb. of marrow.
$\frac{1}{2}$ oz. of yeast to each 2 pints
of liquid.

This is rather an extravagant way of making wine, but as the result is very good perhaps it may be excused.

Take a really ripe marrow and remove the peel and seeds. Weigh the remainder and cut the flesh into tiny pieces; you may put it through the mincer if you wish. Place in a large bowl, and allowing 1 lb. of sugar to each 2 lb. of marrow, cover the marrow with demerara sugar.

Cover the bowl and leave for a week, when you will find the sugar has dissolved and extracted the juice from the marrow. Strain the liquid off into a bowl and add the lemon juice, half a lemon to each pint of liquid. Stir in the yeast, $\frac{1}{2}$ oz. to two pints of liquid. Cover the bowl and leave for three days, stir daily.

It is then ready to bottle. This wine will need feeding with sugar candy every two or three weeks until fermentation has finished. Try to leave it about nine months at least before drinking as this wine greatly improves with age.

MARROW WHISKY

4 lb. ripe marrow.
3 lb. demerara sugar.
½ lb. raisins.
Juice of one lemon.
1 oz. yeast.
1 gallon water.

Take 4 lb. of ripe marrow and remove the pith and seeds but do not peel. Cut it into small pieces and put in a saucepan with ½ lb. of raisins and a gallon of cold water. Bring to the boil and simmer till the marrow is tender, add some more water if it evaporates too much.

Put the 3 lb. of demerara sugar in a large bowl and strain the liquid on to it, add the juice of one lemon. Stir till the sugar has dissolved and when the liquid is lukewarm stir in the ounce of yeast.

Cover the bowl and leave for four days, stirring daily. Then bottle it, but cork very loosely at first. This wine will need feeding with sugar candy every two or three weeks. After about six weeks you may find a thick sediment at the bottom of the bottle, strain this off and add some more sugar to the bottle. Keep a spare bottle to bring the wine to the top of the bottle again.

Ready in six months but much better if you can keep it longer. It is very good!

MARROW RUM

> 1 ripe marrow.
> About 5 to 7 lb. of demerara
>   sugar according to the size
>   of the marrow.

Choose a really ripe marrow, wipe it clean with a damp cloth, then cut a piece off the stalk end of the marrow, deep enough to enable you to scoop out the seeds and pith, from the rest of the marrow. Press the demerara sugar into the cavity left; it depends on the size of the marrow how much you will need; a large one will take about seven pounds of sugar.

Replace the end of the marrow and seal with a piece of sticky tape. Then suspend the marrow over a jar or jug; something with a narrow neck so that the marrow can rest on this but not touch the bottom of the container.

After two or three weeks unseal the end of the marrow and add some more sugar; some of the first lot will have been absorbed into the flesh of the marrow. Put the end on again and leave for about six or seven weeks, when the sugar should have mixed with the flesh of the marrow and the resulting liquid will have dripped through into the jar leaving only the shell of the marrow.

Bottle the liquid; if you have a stone jar use that. Cork loosely at first. Keep the wine at least twelve months, when it will be very strong, very much like rum.

MULBERRY WINE

4 lb. mulberries.
3½ lb. granulated sugar.
1 gallon water.

The mulberries are best picked before they are quite ripe. Wash them and put them into a large bowl. Crush the berries with a wooden spoon, then pour over hem a gallon of boiling water, and stir well.

Cover the bowl and leave it for five days, stir well daily. After five days strain the liquid off the fruit into another bowl or jug and add the 3½ lb. of granulated sugar. Stir well till the sugar has dissolved then cover the bowl and leave for another three days; stir daily.

The wine is now ready to bottle. Cork the bottles loosely at first and keep them if possible in a cool dark place. Inspect them every day or so to see that the corks are still in, the wine may ferment and push the corks out. If this happens you will probably have to fill up the bottles again, so keep a spare bottle for this purpose.

Push the corks in when fermentation has finished and keep the wine at least a year before drinking; the longer you keep it the better it will be.

ORANGE WINE

> 4 lb. over-ripe oranges.
> 3 lb. loaf sugar.
> 1 gallon boiling water.

The oranges must be really over-ripe; it doesn't matter if they are mouldy, the wine will be all the better. The greengrocer will usually part with these quite cheaply; he may even give them to you; mine does.

Slice the oranges into a large bowl and pour over them a gallon of boiling water. Stir them well then cover the bowl and leave for two weeks without stirring. There should be a good mould on top by this time if the oranges were nice and mouldy.

Remove the mould carefully without breaking it if possible, then strain the liquid off into another bowl. Add 3 lb. of loaf sugar and stir till it has dissolved, then cover the bowl and leave for four days but stir daily. The wine is now ready to bottle.

You may need to add some sugar candy to each bottle after about a month; taste the wine; if it is still sweet then leave it alone.

Keep the wine for a year before drinking as it will then be at its best. This really is a lovely wine and very strong. It is a great favourite with many people.

PARSNIP WINE. FIRST METHOD

4 lb. parsnips.
3½ lb. loaf sugar.
1 lemon.
½ oz. yeast.
1½ gallons cold water.

This wine is best made in February or March with parsnips which have remained in the ground all the winter.

Scrub the parsnips well but do not peel them; slice them thinly and put them in a large saucepan or preserving pan. Pour in 1½ gallons of cold water, if you haven't a saucepan big enough, cook 2 lb. of parsnips and ¾ of a gallon of water at a time. When they are cooked strain the liquid off into the same bowl. Cook the parsnips till they are tender but not mashy.

After straining throw away the parsnips and return the liquid to the pan. Add 3½ lb. loaf sugar and the lemon sliced thinly, simmer for three-quarters of an hour, stir occasionally. Strain again into a large bowl, and when lukewarm stir in ½ oz. of yeast.

Cover the bowl and leave for four days, then stir it well and bottle. Cork loosely at first. The wine will be drinkable in six months, but much better if you can leave it longer. You may need to add some sugar or sugar candy after a month or so.

PARSNIP WINE. SECOND METHOD

> 4 lb. parsnips.
> 3 lb. demerara sugar.
> ½ oz. hops.
> ½ oz. yeast.
> 1½ gallons cold water.

Scrub the parsnips well without peeling them and slice thinly into a large saucepan or preserving pan. Pour on 1½ gallons of water and bring to the boil, simmer till the parsnips are tender but not mashy. Now add ½ oz. of hops and simmer for about half an hour.

Put 3 lb. of demerara sugar into a bowl and strain the liquid on to it, stir well and leave till it is lukewarm. Spread ½ oz. of yeast on a piece of toast and float on top, cover the bowl and leave it for twelve to fourteen days.

Remove the toast and strain again if necessary, then bottle. Cork loosely at first and be ready to fill up if the wine ferments over the top of the bottles. Add some demerara sugar or sugar candy at intervals of about two weeks, until the wine has finished working.

I think the hops give rather an unpleasant bitter taste when the wine is new, but leave it a year or more and then it's a wonderful wine.

PEAR WINE

> 5 lb. ripe pears.
> 3 lb. granulated sugar.
> 1 gallon cold water.
> $\frac{1}{2}$ oz. yeast.

The pears must be very ripe; even the squashy ones will do; this is a good way of using them as pears do go soft so quickly.

Wash the pears or wipe them well with a damp cloth. Do not peel or core them, but cut them in pieces into a large saucepan or preserving pan, and pour on a gallon of cold water. Bring them slowly to the boil, and simmer gently for about half an hour.

Strain the liquid off through muslin into a large bowl, and add 3 lb. of granulated sugar and the yeast, stir till it has dissolved. Use a wooden spoon for stirring. Cover the bowl and stir daily for three days. Then bottle.

Put a piece of sugar candy into each bottle as you fill it. Cork loosely at first, and gradually push the corks in further as fermentation slows down. When the wine is still, no more sizzling noises or bubbles rising when you move the bottle, then it is safe to cork it tightly.

Keep the wine nine months or more before drinking. Store it in a cool dark place if possible.

FRESH PEACH WINE

3 lb. peaches.
3½ lb. granulated sugar.
½ oz. yeast.
1 gallon boiling water.

Choose ripe peaches, wipe them with a damp cloth and cut them in half to remove the stones. Then put the 3 lb. of peaches in a large bowl, pour over a gallon of boiling water and stir them well with a wooden spoon. Cover the bowl and stir daily for three days, then leave it covered without stirring for a week.

After a week strain the liquid off into another bowl and add to it 3½ lb. of sugar and ½ oz. of yeast. Stir well till the sugar has dissolved then cover the bowl and leave for a week, stirring daily. It is now ready to bottle.

Cork the bottles loosely at first, and after two weeks add a little sugar candy to each bottle. When you are sure the wine has finished working push the corks in tight. The wine should not need any more sugar candy added if you have used the correct amount of yeast— not more than ½ oz. Too much will keep consuming the sugar and may in the end turn the wine sour.

The wine is ready to drink in six months.

DRIED PEACH WINE

> 2 lb. dried peaches.
> 3½ lb. granulated sugar.
> ½ oz. yeast.
> 1 gallon cold water.

Soak 2 lb. of peaches for twelve hours in a gallon of cold water. Then place peaches and water in a large saucepan or preserving pan and bring to the boil, simmer for a few minutes. Strain the liquid off into a bowl and add 3½ lb. granulated sugar, stir well till the sugar has dissolved. When the liquid is lukewarm stir in the ½ oz. of yeast. Cover the bowl and stand for four days, stirring daily. Then the wine is ready to bottle. Add some sugar candy to each bottle after three weeks. Cork loosely till fermentation has finished.

The wine should be ready to drink in about nine months.

Don't throw away the peaches after you have strained off the liquid; with some sugar added they will make jam. Put the peaches with a little water in a saucepan and add about four pounds of sugar, then make the jam in the usual way. To save you looking it up, that is stir over a low heat till the sugar has melted, then boil quickly until a little jam dropped on a cold plate wrinkles when the plate is tilted.

PLUM WINE

3½ lb. ripe plums.
4 lb. granulated sugar.
¼ oz. yeast.
1 gallon boiling water.

Choose really ripe plums, any kind will do. Pick off all stalks and leaves and wash the plums or wipe them with a damp cloth. Put them in a large bowl and pour over a gallon of water, stir and mash them with a wooden spoon, then cover the bowl and leave for ten days.

There will probably be a mould on top by this time, remove this carefully; try not to break any off into the liquid. Strain the liquid off the plums into another bowl and add 4 lb. of granulated sugar and ¼ oz. of yeast then stir well till the sugar has dissolved. Cover the bowl but stir daily for three days.

The wine is then ready to bottle. Cork it loosely at first and see that the corks stop in. The wine should be ready to drink in six months.

You may if you use really over-ripe plums leave out the yeast, the wine will be as good but will take longer to mature, so leave it at least nine months, and of course longer if you can.

POTATO WINE. FIRST METHOD

4 lb. old potatoes.
3 lb. demerera sugar.
1 lemon.
1 orange.
Small piece of root
   ginger.
1 oz. yeast.
1½ gallons cold water.

Wash the potatoes well but do not peel them. Cut them into small pieces and put into a large saucepan or preserving pan, with 1½ gallons of water. If your pan won't hold this amount put in as much as you can and add the rest as the water evaporates. Boil the potatoes till they are soft but not mashy.

Strain off the liquid into a large bowl, and add the 3 lb. demerera sugar, the sliced orange and lemon and the piece of root ginger. Stir this well till the sugar has dissolved then return the liquid to the pan and simmer for half an hour.

Now pour the liquid back into the bowl and wait till it is lukewarm, then spread the ounce of yeast on a piece of toast and float on top.

Cover the bowl and leave it for three days. After this time remove the piece of toast and strain the wine again then bottle it. Add some sugar candy after four weeks; ready in six months.

POTATO WINE. SECOND METHOD

3 lb. old potatoes.

1 lb. raisins.

4 lb. demerara sugar.

½ oz. hops.

½ oz. yeast.

1 gallon boiling water.

Wash the potatoes but do not peel them. Cut them into small pieces and put them in a large bowl. Add 4 lb. demerara sugar, 1 lb. of raisins and ½ oz. of hops, pour over them a gallon of boiling water and stir well with a wooden spoon.

When the contents of the bowl are lukewarm stir in ½ oz. of yeast. Cover the bowl and leave for two weeks, stirring daily. After two weeks strain the liquid off through muslin and bottle.

Cork loosely at first, have some wine in a spare bottle to fill the bottles if the wine should ferment over the top. Add some sugar candy to each bottle at intervals of about three weeks until fermentation has finished. You will realise that fermentation has finished when you add a piece of sugar candy to a bottle and the wine remains clear, does not bubble or fizz; this means that the yeast has finished working and cannot absorb any more sugar. The wine should be ready in six months.

PRUNE WINE

1½ lb. prunes.
3 lb. demerara sugar.
½ lb. raisins.
½ oz. yeast.
1 gallon cold water.

Wash the prunes and put them in a bowl with enough water to cover them and allow for swelling. Soak the prunes for twelve hours, then tip them into a saucepan or preserving pan and add enough water to make it up to a gallon.

Cut the raisins into small pieces and add to the prunes, then bring them to the boil and simmer for about half an hour. Mash the prunes while they are cooking with a wooden spoon. After half an hour strain off the liquid into a bowl and add the 3 lb. of demerara sugar, stir till the sugar has dissolved.

When the liquid is lukewarm stir in ½ oz. of yeast. Cover the bowl and leave it to stand for five days, stirring daily. It is then ready to bottle.

Cork loosely at first and fill up if the wine oozes over the top. You may find it needs a little sugar or sugar candy added after a month or so, but if it tastes sweet leave it alone and cork it down tightly when you are sure it has finished working.

QUINCE WINE

3 lb. ripe quinces.
3½ lb. granulated sugar.
1 gallon cold water.

Wash the quinces and cut into four, but do not remove the cores as they will improve the flavour of the wine.

Put the quinces in a large bowl, and pour over them 1 gallon of cold water. Cover the bowl and leave them to stand for seven days.

When the seven days are up, strain off the liquid into another bowl and add 3½ lb. of granulated sugar. Stir well with a wooden spoon till the sugar has dissolved, then cover the bowl and leave for another three days but stir daily.

The wine is then ready. Put the corks in loosely at first and look every day or so to see that they haven't popped out. Push the corks in when there are no more signs of the wine working. Store the bottles in as cool and dark a place as you can find.

The wine should be ready to drink in nine months, but if you want to keep it longer it will be all the better for it.

RAISIN WINE

3 lb. raisins (large ones).
3 lb. granulated sugar.
1 orange.
1 lemon.
1 gallon boiling water.
$\frac{1}{4}$ oz. yeast.

Cut up 3 lb. of raisins and put in a bowl with the thinly sliced orange and lemon. Pour on a gallon of boiling water and stir well with a wooden spoon, then cover the bowl. Leave for ten days.

Strain the liquid carefully through muslin into another bowl and stir in 3 lb. of granulated sugar and the $\frac{1}{4}$ oz. of yeast. Stir till the sugar has dissolved then cover the bowl and leave for another ten days, stirring daily.

Next strain again and then bottle the wine. Cork loosely at first and look every day or so to see that the corks are still in. You may find that the wine seems a bit dry after a few weeks as if it needs more sugar, add some or a piece of sugar candy to each bottle. If the wine fizzes when you put the sugar in, it needs some badly.

The wine should be ready to drink in six months but it will improve if you leave it longer.

RASPBERRY WINE

3½ lb. raspberries.
3½ lb. granulated sugar.
1 gallon boiling water.
¼ oz. yeast (the wine can
   be made without this).

Pick or buy the raspberries, it does not matter if they are a bit over-ripe, but wash them well to remove any maggots. I find it best to lay them in a bowl of cold water and swish them about gently; if there are any maggots they will float to the top.

Place the raspberries in a large bowl, and pour over a gallon of boiling water. Stir them well with a wooden spoon then cover the bowl and leave for ten days.

After the ten days, strain the liquid off the raspberries into another bowl and stir in 3½ lb. of granulated sugar.

Now if you want the wine to age quickly you may add a very little yeast, about a ¼ oz. Stir this in with the sugar, the wine will be quite successful without yeast, only taking longer to mature.

After adding the sugar and yeast, cover the bowl and leave for another five days. Then bottle it. Cork loosely at first and fill up if the wine comes over the top of the bottle. The wine will be ready in six months with yeast and nine months without.

RED CURRANT WINE

> 3 lb. red currants.
> 4 lb. granulated sugar.
> 1 gallon boiling water.

Strip the red currants from the stalks, and put them in a large bowl.   Pour over them a gallon of boiling water and stir well with a wooden spoon.   Cover the bowl and leave it for ten days.

Now strain the liquid off through muslin into another bowl, and add 4 lb. of granulated sugar, stir well till the sugar has dissolved, then cover the bowl and leave for another three days, but stir daily.

After the three days it is ready to bottle.   Cork loosely at first, and see that the corks stay in as red currant wine is inclined to turn sharp very quickly if too much air gets into the bottles.

The wine shouldn't need any more sugar but taste it after a few weeks and add some sugar or sugar candy if it tastes sour.

Keep some of the wine in a small bottle to fill up the bottles if the wine should ferment over the tops.   Push the corks in tight when there are no more signs of the wine working.

Red currant wine should be ready to drink in nine months, but it will improve immensely if kept longer.

RHUBARB WINE. FIRST METHOD

> 3 lb. rhubarb.
> 3 lb. granulated sugar.
> 1 gallon boiling water.

Rhubarb wine should be made in May or June. Choose big sticks if possible, it doesn't matter if it is a bit tough.

Wipe the rhubarb with a damp cloth and cut it into small pieces. Place these in a large bowl and pour on a gallon of boiling water, stir it up well, then cover the bowl and leave for ten days.

You will probably find a mould formed by now; remove this carefully without breaking it into the wine, this is easy if the mould is thick. Strain the liquid off into another bowl, add 3 lb. of granulated sugar and stir well. Cover the bowl and leave for another three days stirring daily.

It is then ready to bottle, cork loosely at first and look fairly often to see that the corks are still in. Push them in when you are sure fermentation has finished.

This wine shouldn't really need sugar added, but I think it is safer to taste it after a few weeks and add a little if it tastes sharp. It depends a great deal on the ripeness of the rhubarb. You can start to drink it after six months.

RHUBARB WINE. SECOND METHOD

```
3 lb. rhubarb.
3 lb. granulated sugar.
1 gallon cold water.
¼ oz. yeast.
```

Some people prefer to make their rhubarb wine by this method. Wipe the rhubarb with a damp cloth and cut it into small pieces, put them into a large bowl and bruise them well. Pour on a gallon of cold water and stir for a few minutes with a wooden spoon, then cover the bowl and leave it for ten days.

Next remove any mould, and strain off the liquid through muslin into another bowl. Stir in the 3 lb. of granulated sugar and ¼ oz. of yeast then cover the bowl and leave for four days, but this time stir daily. Strain again and bottle.

Cork loosely at first, and have that spare bottle handy to fill up. Add a good size lump of sugar candy to each bottle after about two months. This will probably liven up the fermentation for a bit, but when the wine is clear and still, tighten the corks.

The wine is ready in six months, but will improve if you keep it longer. Rhubarb wine turns out to be a rather dry wine, very clear and sparkling. It is one of my favourites.

RICE WINE

3 lb. rice.
3 lb. granulated sugar.
1 oz. yeast.
1 lb. large raisins.
1 lemon.
1 gallon warm water.

Cut the raisins in half, and place in a bowl with the 3 lb. of rice and 3 lb. granulated sugar. Squeeze the juice from the lemon and add it to these. Now pour on a gallon of warm water and stir well.

Mix the ounce of yeast with a little warm water till it is creamy, then mix with the other ingredients and stir well with a wooden spoon. Cover the bowl and stand in a warm place for three days, stirring daily, then leave for another eight days without stirring.

After eight days remove the scum from the top and strain the liquid off into bottles. Cork very loosely at first and fill up from a spare bottle if the wine ferments over the tops of the bottles. Drop a piece of sugar candy into each bottle every three or four weeks; when the wine doesn't fizz or bubble as you drop it in you will know that fermentation has finished and the wine doesn't want more feeding.

Keep the wine for at least six months, or longer if you can.

SLOE WINE

3½ lb. sloes.
3½ lb. sugar.
1 gallon boiling water.

The sloes are best picked after a frost, usually about the end of September or the beginning of October.

Gather 3½ lb. of sloes and wash them well. Place them in a large bowl and pour on one gallon of boiling water. Stir them round for a bit, then cover the bowl and leave it to stand till a thick mould has formed over the sloes. It may take weeks or even months, but it doesn't matter how long they stand. The thicker the mould the better the wine.

Lift the mould off carefully without breaking it if possible, then strain off the liquid through muslin, into another bowl. Stir in 3½ lb. of granulated sugar and cover the bowl; then leave for five days, but stir daily. It is then ready to bottle.

It seems to depend on the time this wine is made as to whether it will need sugar added; I have made two lots within a week of each other and found that one needed sugar after a few weeks and the other was still quite sweet. So taste it and add some if you think it needs more sugar. But remember that all wines lose a certain amount of sweetness as they mature. Try to keep the wine a year before drinking.

STRAWBERRY WINE

4 lb. ripe strawberries.
3 lb. loaf sugar.
1 gallon boiling water.
1 lemon.

Use ripe strawberries, it matters not if they are squashy. Remove the hulls and wash the strawberries to get rid of any earth or dust.

Place them in a large bowl with the juice of a lemon and pour over a gallon of boiling water. With a wooden spoon mash the strawberries and stir well, then cover the bowl and leave for a week.

Strain the juice off carefully into another bowl, don't squeeze any of the pulp through the muslin, and add the 3 lb. of loaf sugar. Stir till this has dissolved, then cover the bowl again and leave for three days, but stir daily.

Now it is ready to bottle, cork loosely and wait till there are no sizzling noises or bubbles rising before pushing the corks in tight.

Store the wine in a cool dark place and keep it at least six months before drinking, except of course for tasting at intervals; I always taste mine to see how it is going on and if it needs any more sugar. It is quite a job tasting several dozen bottles though.

SUGAR BEET WINE

4 lb. sugar beet.
3 lb. loaf sugar.
1 lemon.
½ oz. yeast.
1½ gallons cold water.

Scrub the sugar beet well but do not peel. Slice thinly into a large saucepan or preserving pan and add 1½ gallons of cold water. If your saucepan won't hold this amount put some in and add more as the liquid in the pan evaporates.

Bring to the boil and simmer gently till the beet is tender. Then strain the liquid off through muslin into a bowl or jug and throw away the beet. Return the liquid to the pan and add 3 lb. of loaf sugar and a thinly sliced lemon; boil for half an hour then strain off into a bowl and leave till lukewarm.

Now stir in ½ oz. of yeast, cover the bowl and leave for six days, stirring daily. Then strain and bottle. Put the corks in loosely at first, and push them down as fermentation finishes. Add a piece of sugar candy to each bottle after a month. Fill the bottles from a spare bottle if the level goes down, as it sometimes does when wine is fermenting.

Keep the wine in a cool dark place for at least nine months, when it should be ready to drink.

TEA WINE

4 pints cold tea.
2 lb. granulated sugar.
½ lb. raisins.
2 lemons.

Cut up the raisins and slice the lemons thinly, and put them in a large bowl or jug. Add 2 lb. of granulated sugar, then pour on four pints of cold tea. Stir till the sugar has dissolved then cover the bowl or jug and leave it for a month.

After this time you will find a scum on top, remove this carefully, then strain off the liquid and bottle.

Tea wine can be drunk at once, but I think it is best when kept a few months. Keep it in a cool dark place, and don't push the corks in too hard at first.

It sounds strange to make wine from tea, but it does turn out a good wine, tasting not in the least like tea. Of course there is no need to make tea especially for this purpose, if you usually throw away half a pot of tea as I think most people do, just save this till you have four pints, strain off the tea leaves though.

I suppose the different kinds of tea and the strength of the brew must make some difference to the wine, so yours will probably turn out differently to your neighbour's.

81

TOMATO WINE

6 lb. ripe tomatoes.
2 lb. granulated sugar.
$\frac{1}{2}$ teaspoon salt.
$\frac{1}{2}$ gallon boiling water.

Cut up the tomatoes with a stainless steel knife, or one of those little plastic saw edged knives which do the job so well. Place the cut tomatoes in a piece of butter muslin and squeeze the juice through into a basin. Pour this over the 2 lb. of granulated sugar in a large bowl, add the $\frac{1}{2}$ teaspoon of salt and pour over half a gallon of boiling water.

Stir well till the sugar has dissolved, then cover the bowl and leave for three days. Strain if necessary and bottle.

Cork the bottles loosely at first, and keep some of the tomato wine in a small bottle to fill up the bottles if the wine should ferment over the top.

When the wine is clear and still, no signs of bubbling or hissing noises, then it is safe to push the corks in tightly. Store them in a cool dark place if possible, anyway in the coolest darkest cupboard you possess.

Keep tomato wine a year or more before you attempt to drink it.

TURNIP WINE. FIRST METHOD

4 lb. turnips.
3½ lb. loaf sugar.
1 lemon.
1 orange.
½ oz. yeast.
1½ gallons cold water.

Scrub the turnips well but do not peel them, slice thinly into a large saucepan or preserving pan. Pour in 1½ gallons of water or as much as the pan will hold, you can add some more as the liquid evaporates in the pan.

Bring to the boil and simmer till the turnips are tender but not mashy. Strain off the liquid into a bowl and throw away the turnips. Put the liquid back in the pan, add a thinly sliced orange and lemon, and 3½ lb. of loaf sugar. Simmer for another half an hour then strain the liquid through muslin into a bowl. When it is lukewarm add ½ oz. of yeast, stir it in well.

Cover the bowl and leave for four days, stir daily, then strain again if necessary and bottle. Cork the bottles very loosely at first, and fill them up if the wine oozes out of the tops. Add a piece of sugar candy to each bottle after three weeks.

The wine is ready in six months, but improves greatly with age.

TURNIP WINE. SECOND METHOD

```
4 lb. turnips.
3 lb. demerara sugar.
½ oz. hops.
½ oz. yeast.
1½ gallons cold water.
```

Scrub the turnips but do not peel them. Slice them thinly into a saucepan or preserving pan and pour on 1½ gallons of cold water. Bring to the boil and simmer til the turnips are tender, then add the ½ oz. of hops and simmer for another half an hour. I warn you the place will smell like a brewery while these are cooking.

Strain the liquid off through muslin into a bowl, and add the sugar. Stir well till the sugar has dissolved. When the liquid is lukewarm spread the ½ oz. of yeast on a slice of toast and float on top.

Cover the bowl and leave for twelve to fourteen days. Then remove the toast, strain and bottle. As usual cork loosely till fermentation has finished, and keep the bottles filled.

The turnips taste very strongly and the hops give the wine a bitter flavour at first, but this wears off and the wine is very good if you can leave it nine months or a year. It will probably need some sugar candy added after a month or so, if you are not sure, it won't hurt to drop a piece in each bottle.

WHEAT WHISKY. FIRST METHOD

2 lb. sultanas.
1 pint wheat.
1 lb. barley.
2 large potatoes
  (finely grated).
4 lb. demerera sugar.
1 gallon tepid water.

Peel the two large potatoes and grate them finely into a large bowl. Add the pint of wheat, 1 lb. of barley, 2 lb. sultanas and 4 lb. of demerera sugar. Pour on a gallon of tepid water and stir well till the sugar has dissolved.

Cover the bowl and leave for three weeks, but stir daily. Then strain the liquid off through muslin and bottle. Cork the bottles loosely at first, and fill the bottles if the wine ferments over the top.

After about a month add a piece of sugar candy about the size of a walnut to each bottle, you will have to break the candy into smaller pieces of course to get it in. Add some more after another month.

When you are sure that fermentation has finished cork the bottles tightly and leave for at least nine months, much longer if you can, as this is a wine that improves immensely with age. It becomes very much like whisky as it matures.

WHEAT WHISKY. SECOND METHOD

1 pint of wheat.

2 lb. sultanas.

2 large potatoes
(finely grated).

4 lb. demerara sugar.

1 oz. yeast.

Grated rind and juice of
two lemons.

1 gallon tepid water.

Peel the potatoes and grate very finely into a large bowl.
Add the pint of wheat, 2 lb. sultanas, 4 lb. demerara
sugar, the grated rind and juice of two lemons, no pith,
and 1 oz. of yeast.

Pour on a gallon of tepid water and mix very thoroughly
with a wooden spoon. Cover the bowl and stand for
three weeks, stirring daily.

After the three weeks strain off the wine carefully
through muslin and bottle. Put the corks in loosely at
first, the wine will probably ferment over the tops of the
bottles so keep them filled, and put the corks back as
they are pushed out.

Add some sugar candy to each bottle at intervals of
about three weeks until the wine doesn't fizz after you have
dropped it in. When you are sure that the wine has
finished fermenting push the corks in tight.

Keep for six months or longer.

WHEAT WINE

1½ lb. wheat.

3 lb. granulated sugar.

1 lemon.

1 orange.

½ teaspoon ground ginger.

½ oz. yeast.

1½ gallons cold water.

Put the 1½ lb. of wheat in a large saucepan or preserving pan with 1½ gallons of cold water and bring to the boil. Simmer for half an hour, then strain the liquid into a large bowl. Add 3 lb. of granulated sugar, the sliced orange and lemon and ½ teaspoon of ground ginger, stir well with a wooden spoon.

When the mixture is lukewarm stir in ½ oz. of yeast. Cover the bowl and leave it for fourteen days, stir it occasionally, then strain and bottle.

Cork loosely at first and look every day or so to see that the corks are still in. Keep the bottles filled if the wine oozes over the tops.

Feed the wine with sugar candy every three weeks until the wine is clear with no bubbles rising. Taste it to see how much candy you think it needs. Of course sugar will do if you are unable to obtain sugar candy.

Keep the wine at least six months and much longer if possible.

PART IV

OTHER DRINKS

BLACKBERRY CORDIAL

2 quarts blackberries.
¼ pint cold water.
1 lb. granulated sugar
    to each quart of juice.
8 cloves.
½ nutmeg.
Wineglass of rum or
    brandy.

Wash the blackberries and put them in a thick saucepan with a quarter of a pint of water, simmer very gently till the fruit is mashy. Tip the blackberries into a piece of muslin and squeeze all the juice out, into a bowl. Measure the juice, and to each quart allow a pound of granulated sugar.

Put the juice and sugar into the saucepan and add eight cloves and half a nutmeg, not grated. Boil for half an hour stirring all the time, skim off any scum that forms.

Take the saucepan off the heat and add a wineglass of rum or brandy. Let the cordial cool a little then pour into warm bottles, put the corks in tightly and to make sure the cordial will keep, seal the bottle with wax.

This is a very good drink for preventing or curing colds and chills—take a wineglass when necessary.

GINGER BEER

> 1 oz. root ginger.
> 1 lb. loaf sugar.
> ½ oz. cream of tartar.
> ½ oz. compressed yeast.
> 2 lemons.
> 2 teaspoons caster sugar.
> 1 gallon boiling water.

Bruise the root ginger and put it in a large bowl with the pound of loaf sugar and ½ an ounce of cream of tartar. Wash the lemons and peel off the yellow rind very thinly, then remove the pith and slice the remainder of the lemons. Add the peel and lemon slices to the ginger, sugar and cream of tartar and pour over a gallon of boiling water.

Stir very well with a wooden spoon, then leave to become lukewarm. Cream the ½ ounce of yeast with the two teaspoons of caster sugar and add to the other ingredients, stir well. I use ordinary baker's yeast and find it works as well as compressed yeast.

Cover the bowl and leave for one day, then strain and bottle. Use screw top bottles or tie the corks on. The ginger beer will be ready to drink in three days, it pops and fizzes just like the shop variety, so I am sure it will be popular with the younger folk.

MEAD

3 lb. honey.
2 whites of eggs.
$\frac{1}{4}$ oz. yeast.
1 lemon.
1 gallon cold water.

Put the 3 lb. of honey and grated rind of the lemon in a large saucepan or preserving pan, with one gallon of cold water. Beat the whites of the two eggs till they are frothy and add to the rest of the ingredients.

Place the pan over the heat and stir as the mixture comes to the boil. Then simmer gently for one hour. Pour the liquid into a large bowl and leave it to become lukewarm, then stir in the $\frac{1}{4}$ oz. of yeast.

Cover the bowl and leave in a fairly warm place for three days; stir daily. Then strain through muslin and bottle. Put the corks in loosely and see that they do not work out as the mead ferments. Gradually push them in tighter as the fermentation slows down.

Store the bottles in a cool dark place, and keep the mead at least a year before drinking it, as it improves immensely with keeping.

Not many people drink mead now, but it was a very popular drink in olden times.

CIDER

For the best cider a mixture of different varieties of apples is best. Those usually chosen are non-keepers, small sour or windfalls, with, if desired, a few crab-apples. An odd rotten apple in a large number is permissible, but otherwise they should be sound.

Before the war, there were travelling cider presses in some districts, as many farms and cottages had a small orchard. This practice seems to have ended now though it may continue in a few country areas.

To get your apples pressed ideally, a cider factory is the thing, if you can persuade them to do it. Alternatively, a cider factory might sell you the newly pressed apple juice. For those who cannot find a cider factory there is a fruit press which is supplied by the famous firm of W. R. Loftus Ltd, of 1–3 Charlotte St., London, W.1.

The juice should be put into a wooden cask—a 30 gallon ex-brandy cask is ideal for first class good keeping cider. Base your calculations on the fact that a ton of apples makes approximately 150 gallons of cider, therefore a cwt. makes approximately $7\frac{1}{2}$ gallons. Any good sized wooden cask is suitable but the larger the better as fermentation goes on longer in a greater quantity of juice, thus producing a higher alcohol content. The cask should stand in a cool place either on its side or end, wherever the bung hole is uppermost.

Never bung up the hole while fermentation is still going on; unless to bring the cask home perhaps! After about forty-eight hours the apple juice will start to ferment and white froth bubble up through the bung hole. This will continue for about three weeks. When fermentation has almost stopped some juice should be syphoned out of the cask with a short length of hose. The amount of juice removed should be sufficient to dissolve the required quantity of sugar.

Add 2 to 4 lb. of sugar (depending on how sweet you want the cider) per gallon *in the cask* to the juice you have removed and dissolve over heat. When quite dissolved allow to cool, then return to the cask. Owing to the addition of the sugar there will now be some juice left over. During fermentation, which will go on for about two weeks, the quantity of juice reduces so that you can add gradually (as space permits) the juice which was surplus. When fermentation has nearly finished, if all the "juice and sugar mixture" is not in the cask, syphon out enough juice to allow this to go in. Then bottle surplus and use to keep cask full while cider is maturing— as the quantity reduces during this process and airspace in the cask will allow bacilli to breed and turn cider acid. When the juice has completely ceased to "bubble up" bung the cask up tightly with either cork or wood and leave for eight months.

Cider is usually made in October–November and should be left *as long as possible* up to two years before opening it but at least until the cuckoo sings the following year. Then the cask may be tapped, or the cider bottled down with care.

Innocent to taste but powerful—up to 15% alcohol can be achieved.

BEER

```
Peck malt.
4 oz. hops.
12 gallons water.
½ oz. brewers' or bakers' yeast.
To make about 9 gallons of
    beer.
```

Firstly, I must warn you that it is necessary to have a licence to brew beer. Enquire at your nearest Customs and Excise Office. The cost varies in proportion to the rateable value of your property.

This recipe makes about nine gallons of normal strength beer. If you wish to brew something stronger, cut down the amount of water. If you would like it weaker, then increase the amount of water. To make half the quantity halve the ingredients exactly, and in the same way, if doubling it see that you double all the ingredients and do not forget any.

To make this amount you need a copper to hold a little over twelve gallons of water, otherwise you will have to make it half at a time.

Put the twelve gallons of cold water in the copper, allow a little more, as if it is a copper with a fire underneath it must have some left in to prevent burning. Bring the water to the boil, then pour it into the tub. Leave it until you can see the reflection of your face in the water then gradually add the malt, stirring briskly all the time. Stir for a minute or two, then cover the tub with a cloth to prevent the steam escaping and to draw out the goodness of the malt. Leave for five or six hours.

Now strain the liquid through a straining cloth and put it back in the copper with the four ounces of hops. Bring to the boil and simmer for forty minutes. Then strain it again into the tub and when it is lukewarm add the yeast. This should be brewers' yeast, but if you cannot get this bakers' yeast will have to do, although it is not quite so good. It can be spread on toast or stirred in. Cover the tub again and leave for twenty-four hours. After this time skim the yeast scum off the top of the beer, then pour it into the barrel without straining. It is ready to drink in two weeks.

The barrel must be scrupulously clean; the best ones to use are those that have contained wine, never use a vinegar barrel. Put the tap in the barrel before pouring in the beer, wind a piece of cloth round the tap before knocking it in to prevent leaking. Never bang the tap itself when putting it in; hold a piece of wood over the tap and knock this. After the beer has been poured in the barrel must be bunged up as tight as possible. To make it easier to withdraw the bung to use the barrel again, wrap a piece of clean rag round the bung before knocking it in, leaving the corners outside to pull on when removing the bung.

If the beer does not run properly when drawing it, some air must be let in at the top. Make a hole in the bung and put a little wooden peg in, withdraw this when drawing beer to let the air in and replace it afterwards. The bung must be really secure with no air entering the barrel during the fourteen days before the beer is ready to drink.

Years ago, when most farm-workers made their own beer, the usual thing to do was to use a withe. That is a hazel stick with the bark peeled off and tied as if it was tying a bundle of faggots. This was dropped in the beer when the yeast was put in, it absorbed the yeast and so could be used for the next brew instead of yeast, if the next brew was to be within a week. Or it could be handed on to a fellow worker to save him buying yeast.

Not many people these days brew their own beer, I suppose it is much easier to buy it. The farm-workers of years ago however could not afford to do this on their meagre wages, so to be able to drink beer they were forced to brew their own. There are a few old men left who prefer the flavour of their home brewed beer to that they buy in the "pub".

FRUIT SYRUPS. 7 RECIPES

Fruit syrups make a good base for many summer drinks, or with those such as black currant, excellent winter hot drinks for sore throats and colds. These can be made as the various fruits become available and stored in the same way as bottled fruit.

It is best to use the juicy fruits, as it is unnecessary to add water. Any less juicy fruits require a little water added and boiling to extract the juice.

To make certain the fruit syrups will keep, it is best to sterilise them by the water immersion method, as in bottling fruit. Pour the syrup into a preserving jar, screw on the metal top, then give a half turn back to loosen it. Place this in a saucepan of cold water with a folded cloth underneath and bring slowly to the boil. Boil for about twenty minutes, then remove carefully and stand on a wooden surface or dry folded cloth. Screw the top on tightly and leave to cool.

The syrup will retain its colour and flavour better if it is stored in a dark place. It should keep indefinitely. Once the jar is opened use it up fairly quickly.

BLACKBERRY SYRUP

```
3 pints blackberry juice.
3 lb. granulated sugar.
2 pints water.
```

Pick really ripe blackberries, look them over, remove any stems or hulls and then wash them well.

Place in a saucepan with just enough water to prevent burning—about half a teacup to a pound of fruit. Simmer very gently for twenty minutes then remove from the heat and mash the berries with a wooden spoon. Strain the juice off through a jelly bag or butter muslin into a jug.

Allow three pounds of granulated sugar and two pints of water to every three pints of blackberry juice. Put the sugar and water in a saucepan and bring slowly to the boil, remove any scum, boil for five minutes, then add the blackberry juice and boil for another five minutes. Remove from the heat and allow to cool before bottling. If you intend to use it in a few days it will keep in bottles, but if it is to be kept for some time then it is better to sterilise it (as was done with the previous recipe), otherwise a mould would probably form in the bottle.

Store the syrup in a cool dark place. This syrup is also a great preventative for colds and chills if taken hot.

BLACKCURRANT SYRUP

```
3 pints blackcurrant juice.
3 lb. granulated sugar.
2 pints water.
```

Pick the blackcurrants when ripe, remove the stalks and wash the currants well. Put them in a bowl and mash with a wooden spoon, add some boiling water, about half a teacup to 2 lb. of fruit, mash them again. Then strain the juice off through a jelly bag or muslin.

Measure the juice in a jug, for every three pints of juice allow 3 lb. of granulated sugar and two pints of water. Put the sugar and water in a saucepan and bring it slowly to the boil, skim off any scum that rises. Boil for five minutes, then add the blackcurrant juice and boil for another ten minutes. Remove from the heat and allow to cool before bottling. Pour it into bottles and seal if you only intend to keep it for a short time. But if you wish to keep it some months then it is best to sterilise it in the same way as for bottled fruit. Store it in a dark place.

This syrup is very good for winter coughs and colds, just dilute it to taste in hot or cold water. Also of course it contains vitamin C, which is so necessary to good health, especially for children.

GINGER SYRUP

4 oz. root ginger.
2 pints water.
1 lemon.
1 lb. of granulated sugar
    to every pint of liquid.

Bruise the ginger well—I always break mine into small pieces—and put it with two pints of water in a saucepan; add two or three thin strips of the yellow rind of the lemon. Boil gently for about three quarters of an hour, then strain through muslin into a jug.

For every pint of liquid allow 1 lb. of granulated sugar, put this into a saucepan and add the juice of the lemon. Boil for fifteen minutes, remove the scum as it rises. Leave it to cool then strain and bottle.

Seal the bottles well, or if you intend to keep the syrup for some time pour it into preserving jars and sterilise it. This will then keep for years if it is stored in a cool dark place.

It is a very useful syrup on cold winter days, a little added to a glass of hot water will make a warming drink. It can also be used to flavour cakes and puddings.

LEMON SYRUP

1 pint of lemon juice.
Grated rind of 3 lemons.
3 lb. granulated sugar.
2 pints water.

Wash the lemons and grate the rind from three of them. Squeeze the juice out till you have a pint of juice, if the lemons are warmed first much more juice can be extracted. Put the grated rind and 3 lb. of granulated sugar in a saucepan with two pints of water. Gradually bring this to the boil, stirring all the time, boil for ten minutes and skim if necessary. Pour in the pint of lemon juice and boil for another ten minutes.

Remove the scum and strain the syrup through a jelly bag and leave to cool. When cool pour it into bottles and seal well, or put it in preserving jars and sterilise. Keep the bottles in a cool dark place.

You may wish to make only half this quantity; if you do, be sure to halve the amounts exactly; it is quite easy to forget some of the ingredients and of course this will put the whole recipe out of balance.

ORANGE SYRUP

1 pint orange juice.
Grated rind of 3 oranges.
Grated rind of 1 lemon.
2 pints water.
3 lb. granulated sugar.

Wash the oranges and lemon, grate the rind from three oranges and the one lemon. Squeeze the juice from the oranges until you have a pint, add the juice of the lemon. Mix the grated rind and juice together.

Put the 3 lb. of granulated sugar in a thick saucepan with two pints of cold water and bring it slowly to the boil, boil for five minutes, skimming off any scum that forms. Then add the pint of orange, the lemon juice and grated rind and boil for another fifteen minutes, still removing any scum.

Strain the syrup and when cool pour into bottles and seal well. If you intend to keep the syrup for any length of time it is best to sterilise it in preserving jars.

Keep the bottles in a cool dark place, they will keep for years if sterilised properly. Once a bottle has been opened however it must be used fairly quickly.

RASPBERRY SYRUP

```
1 pint raspberry juice.
1 lb. granulated sugar.
2 tablespoons water.
```

Choose nice ripe raspberries and wash them carefully to remove any maggots; be careful not to lose too much juice while doing this.

Place the raspberries in a saucepan with a thick bottom, with two tablespoons of cold water. Simmer very, very gently till the raspberries are mashy and the juice runs out. Remove them from the heat and mash the berries thoroughly with a wooden spoon. Strain through a jelly bag and measure the liquid into a jug.

For each pint of raspberry juice allow one pound of granulated sugar, return the juice to the saucepan with the sugar and bring to the boil, boil for ten minutes. Remove the scum, strain and while still hot pour into hot bottles and seal.

If you intend to keep the syrup for some time it is safer to pour it into preserving jars and sterilise, in the same way as for bottled fruit.

Keep the bottles in a cool dark place.

STRAWBERRY SYRUP

---

1 pint strawberry juice.
1 lb. granulated sugar.

Pick or buy ripe strawberries, but don't use any bruised ones. Remove the hulls and wash the strawberries, then pack them into large preserving jars and stand these in a saucepan of cold water, place a folded cloth underneath to prevent the jars cracking and bring slowly to the boil. Do not screw the jars down. Boil them till the juice begins to run out, this will not take long, as I have found to my dismay when bottling strawberries.

Remove the jars, remember to stand them on a wooden surface or folded cloth or the jars will crack. Mash the fruit to extract any remaining juice, then strain it all through a jelly bag.

Put the strawberry juice in a saucepan, and for each pint of juice add 1 lb. of granulated sugar. Bring slowly to the boil and boil for fifteen minutes, stirring well all the time. Remove the scum and strain into a bowl and leave till cold. Then pour into preserving jars and sterilise, or if you intend to use it fairly soon, pour it into bottles and seal the tops.

Keep it in a dark place if possible. It is used for summer drinks, with water added.

PART V

CHILDREN'S DRINKS, TEAS
AND COFFEE

———

IT is often a problem to know what to give children to drink in summer. One can buy endless varieties of beverages but they are mostly expensive. I do not think the cheap ones of the gassy type are very good.

I have collected a few recipes, some of which, if they are a little extravagant are more wholesome than the manufactured variety. The others are economical and excellent thirst quenchers.

Children appreciate a drink much more if it is made to look attractive. When sometimes I have only one orange or lemon left, with a little ingenuity I have made it up into some sort of drink, and the children have thought it marvellous because it was pretty.

Milk can be made attractive in the same way. My daughters will not drink plain milk at home, they force it down somehow at school. I think that is mainly because it looks dull. Very often I have added a little cochineal and sugar, called it by some exotic name and it has been swallowed to the last drop, yet the only flavouring was sugar.

I think it especially inviting on a summer day to see a tall glass jug of lemonade, with cool-looking slices of lemon or cucumber floating on top. The floating pieces seem to give it an added charm. I think they have a cooling effect, in the same way as fish swimming in a tank are soothing to watch.

Hot drinks also can be made more appealing by a little deception. My children don't like cocoa made in the usual way; mixed in a cup and hot water poured on, but if I boil it in a saucepan till it is frothy then call it hot chocolate they love it. I hope they do not read this as they will be annoyed to think I have deceived them! It is not the proper thing to do, according to child psycologists. Still chocolate is made from cocoa so perhaps I am right after all.

At party times I always mix a fruit cocktail for the children, so that they don't feel left out of things while the adults are quaffing wine. It is not much trouble and I like any excuse to concoct a new drink.

I have labelled the following drinks as "childrens' drinks" but they need not be confined to children. My husband and I enjoy them too; in fact these are one lot of recipes where they were all willing to act as guinea-pigs!

CHOCOLATE MILK WHIP

2 oz. plain or milk chocolate.
½ pint fresh milk.
Some cream or ice-cream.

This can be made as a hot or cold drink. To make a hot drink put the 2 oz. of chocolate in a pudding basin and stand it in a pan of hot water. Melt it slowly and gradually beat in with a fork the half pint of fresh milk. When the milk is thoroughly beaten in, remove the pan from the heat and using an eggbeater or rotary whisk beat till the mixture is frothy. Pour it into a glass and add a spoonful of cream; do not stir this in.

To make a cold drink, melt the chocolate in the same way, but only beat in a quarter pint of milk. Take the basin out of the saucepan and beat in the rest of the cold milk. Chill thoroughly, then whisk till frothy. Add a spoonful of ice-cream to the glass. Both these recipes can have sugar added to taste. These make very nourishing drinks for invalids or children who will not drink plain milk. I have only given amounts for one glassful, of course the ingredients can be increased in proportion to the number of glasses you require.

CHILDREN'S PARTY SPECIAL

Tin pineapple juice.
Glass lemon squash.
1 pint water.
1 bottle " fizzy " lemonade.
Few glacé or maraschino
   cherries.
Sprigs of mint.
Borage leaves.
1 lemon.

Empty the pineapple juice into a large glass bowl or jug. Add the glass of lemon squash and the pint of cold water and stir well. Pour in a bottle of " fizzy " lemonade —it can be coloured if you like, it makes the drink look gayer. Slice the lemon very thinly and add it; stir the concoction very gently to mix it well. Add the cherries, maraschino or glacé, whichever you have handy, and some sprigs of mint or borage leaves. You can if you like add some pineapple pieces to make it more exciting. Remember to provide spoons as well as drinking straws.

For older children you could alter the recipe a little, squeeze the juice out of the lemon instead of slicing it, and leave out the mint or borage leaves. Serve the drink in small glasses with a cherry on a stick in each.

ECONOMICAL LEMONADE

1 lemon.
$\frac{1}{2}$ lb. granulated sugar.
$\frac{1}{2}$ oz. cream of tartar.
2 quarts of boiling water.
Sprigs of mint.

This is a good cheap lemonade for those with large thirsty families. It is very refreshing on a hot day.

Wash the lemon and slice it thinly, put it into a jug with $\frac{1}{2}$ lb. of granulated sugar and $\frac{1}{2}$ oz. of cream of tartar. Pour over the two quarts of boiling water and stir well with a wooden spoon. Cover the jug and leave it to cool—it is best to leave it overnight.

Pour the lemonade into glass jugs and leave the slices of lemon floating. Wash a few sprigs of mint and add these. Make sure the lemonade is really cold before drinking.

It is a good drink for children's picnics. In the summer mine often ask to have their tea packed to take in the fields, and they like a large bottle of lemonade each and very often one for their friends. Under these conditions one bought bottle is no good at all, unless I am feeling rich and can provide a bottle each. They usually get the home-made variety.

KIDDIES' KOKTAIL

½ pint of any fruit juice.
Tumbler non-alcoholic
      ginger wine.
½ pint coloured lemonade.
Some maraschino cherries.

Any fruit juice will do; that strained off stewed fruit, the juice from a tin of fruit or fresh fruit juice. Fruit syrups mixed with a little water are very good to use.

Put the juice in a jug and pour on the tumbler of non-alcoholic ginger wine, add half a pint of coloured lemonade, match it up to the fruit juice. I find red is the most popular colour. Mix it all thoroughly. Serve in small glasses and to make the children feel quite grown-up put a cherry on a stick in each glass.

My children insist that the type of glass makes the drink taste different—how true—and they will cheerfully fill a small glass many times, rather than save their energy and have one large one. They say the drink is much better in a pretty wine glass. My youngest daughter has even appropriated a small empty champagne bottle, into which she carefully pours her apple wine, and they drink a lot of this when it is new, before transferring it to a glass. To me it seems wasted energy, but perhaps my imagination is not so good.

LEMON BARLEY

2 oz. pearl barley.
1½ pints cold water.
1 lemon.
2 tablespoons sugar.

Put the pearl barley in a saucepan with the 1½ pints of cold water and one or two pieces of lemon peel and simmer for about an hour. Pearl barley seems an awkward kind of thing to cook, the first time I made this I found that if I put the lid on, the water boiled over. I left the lid off and forgot it for more than an hour and found the pearl barley caked in a hard mass on the bottom of the saucepan. So now I compromise; I put the lid half on, and if the liquid seems to be getting dangerously low I add a little more water. Do remember to simmer very gently.

Strain the barley water into a jug and stir in two tablespoons of sugar and the juice of a lemon. Leave it to cool. Dilute to taste and if necessary add some more sugar; it depends whether you have a very sweet tooth.

Do not keep the lemon barley for more than a few days. You may of course use orange juice for flavouring. This is a good beverage for invalids and children as the barley is nourishing and good for your inside.

MARROW CREAM

Ripe marrow.
1 lb. granulated sugar.
1 lemon.
1 pint warm water.
½ oz. yeast.

Cut up about 2 lb. of ripe marrow into very small cubes, omitting the rind and pith. Put the cubes in a bowl and pour over 1 lb. of granulated sugar so that the marrow is all covered. Cover the bowl and leave it over-night.

In the morning you will find the sugar dissolved in the marrow juice; pour this off into a jug. Now over the remaining marrow cubes pour a pint of warm water, stir this for a few minutes then pour off on to the marrow juice.

Add the juice of the lemon and stir in ½ oz. of yeast. Cover the bowl and leave it in a fairly warm place for about half an hour, when you will find it frothy; stir again and it is ready to drink.

It is best drunk while fresh, as if you keep it more than a day or two it will start to turn into wine. This is quite a health giving drink, as both the yeast and lemon contain vitamins and the sugar provides energy.

ORANGE AND LEMON COCKTAIL

2 oranges.
1 lemon.
1½ pints water.
Sugar to taste.
Sprig of mint.
Sprig of borage.
Slices of cucumber.

Cut the oranges in half, and squeeze the juice from one and a half. Cut the lemon in half and squeeze the juice from one half. Cut the remaining halves of orange and lemon into thin slices and put them in the jug with the juice. Add some sugar, about two or three tablespoons according to your taste. Pour on a quarter of a pint of hot water and stir well till the sugar has dissolved, then gradually add the 1¼ pints of cold water.

Float a few sprigs of mint and borage leaves on top, and slide some long strips of cucumber peel down the sides of the jug; use a glass one. Chill thoroughly before serving. If you haven't a refrigerator, stand the jug in a bowl of cold water and cover with a damp cloth, stand the bowl on the floor in a draught.

The mint and borage give it an unusual flavour very summery and refreshing. The children think it is a lovely drink, and it looks attractive with the orange and lemon slices and mint sprigs floating on top.

POPPETS' PUNCH

½ pint any fruit juice from
stewed fruit or fruit syrup
made up to half a pint
with water.
Bottle lemonade.
Some maraschino cherries.
Ice-cream.
Tinned fruit.

The fruit juice can be any strained off stewed fruit;
see that there are no bits floating, or make up some fruit
syrup with water to half a pint.

Put the half a pint of fruit juice in a quart jug and pour
on a bottle of lemonade. Match up the colour and
flavour of the fruit juice with one of the proprietary brands
of fizzy drinks or use plain bottled lemonade. Mix well
then drop in a few maraschino cherries, glacé cherries
will do. Add a spoonful of ice-cream to each glass and
don't forget a cherry for each one.

To make it more of a party drink, make double the
quantity and put it in a large glass bowl, float pieces of
tinned fruit in it, such as pineapple or peaches. Serve
it with a ladle and add a spoonful of ice-cream to each
glass. Provide each glass with a long spoon and drinking
straw.

For a winter party you could leave out the ice-cream,
but I think children enjoy ice-cream whatever the
weather.

STRAWBERRY MILK SHAKE

½ lb. of strawberries.
1 pint of fresh milk.
2 tablespoons of ice-cream.
1 tablespoon of caster sugar
    or glucose.

Wash the strawberries and pick out two of the best looking and put aside. Lay a piece of muslin in a pudding basin and place the rest of the strawberries in this. Mash them well with a wooden spoon, then lift the corners of the muslin and squeeze the juice and as much of the pulp as possible through into the basin.

Sprinkle on to this a tablespoon of caster sugar, or if you wish it to be more energising a heaped tablespoon of glucose; this does not sweeten as much as sugar. Beat this in with a fork and gradually add the fresh milk, then use a whisk and whisk till it is frothy.

Pour this into two tall glasses, add a tablespoon of ice-cream and perch a strawberry on top. Provide a long spoon and a straw. If the drink is not very pink add a few drops of cochineal while whisking.

If you grow strawberries this is not an expensive drink and it is one way of getting children to drink milk. I find if milk is merely coloured and sweetened children are more eager to drink it.

ORANGE REFRESHER

1 orange.
Tumbler orange squash.
1½ pints water.
Sprigs of mint.
Cucumber peel.
1 tablespoon sugar.

Put the tumbler of orange squash in a large jug with the one and a half pints of water. Squeeze the juice from half the orange and add to this, cut the other half into thin slices and float on top.

Stir in a tablespoon of sugar and drop in a few sprigs of mint. Cut a few strips of peel from a cucumber and slide down the side of the jug. Cool thoroughly before drinking. The cucumber and mint give it an added flavour.

You can of course use lemon squash and a lemon if you prefer it, or grapefruit. Another way is to mix them; use half of each squash and either half each of the orange or lemon, or use both and add some more water.

If you possess a refrigerator then a few lumps of ice dropped in make it much more refreshing on a hot day. A good cooling mixture to use if you are not lucky enough to have a frig. is a handful of washing soda and a handful of cooking salt in a little water, stand the jug in this for a while.

HERB TEAS

I expect quite a number of you grow herbs in your gardens, especially the common ones such as mint, sage, thyme and marjoram. These if made into tea all have some special medicinal property, known for hundreds of years by the gypsies and country folk.

I have tried some and they certainly do work. They are not all very pleasant to taste, but I find if one sips them while very hot the flavour is not so pronounced.

Some leaves and flowers of other plants are also used in this way, most are made by pouring hot water on the fresh or dried leaves and leaving the brew to stand for a few minutes in the same way as ordinary tea.

So after reading the following recipes and their healing properties you can go and search in the garden for the cure for your special ailment, and save on chemist's bills. Of one thing you can be sure, if they do not bring relief they can do no harm. I am the guinea pig in this family; if I survive and have no ill effects from drinking a new concoction, then the others will consent to try my wonderful mixtures, that is if they do not taste too horrible.

The children quite like taking the coltsfoot cough mixture, as the honey and lemon disguise the taste of the coltsfoot leaves. Do not try to keep this too long; I bottled some once and forgot it for a while; when I next looked it had turned into wine, but I didn't like it much. So you see almost anything will make wine; I have heard of people using vegetable peelings. But I am wandering from the subject.

There are a great many other herbs found growing wild, which at one time where used as medicines, and many are still used as the basis of modern medicines; but as they would need a book on their own we will keep to the ones which most of us know.

Some of the herbs, such as sage and thyme are ever-green, but I always dry some. With things like mint which just disappear in winter it is imperative to dry enough for winter use, unless you can grow it in a greenhouse or in pots indoors. It is so much easier to take them from a jar in winter than trample round a muddy or snow-covered garden picking what you need.

The most usual way of drying herbs is to hang them in bunches in a warm room and leave them to dry. I think they get dusty this way. I wash mine and dab the leaves dry on a cloth, then spread them out on tins and dry slowly in an oven, electric setting 200 degrees. It takes hours and one must be careful not to over dry them. Leave the oven door open slightly to let the moisture escape quickly. When they are dry the leaves can easily be stripped from the stalks and stored in screw top jars.

I keep one jar of mixed herbs for cooking, ready for stuffing or any other savoury; it saves getting out a whole array of jars and taking a little from each. The home grown herbs smell so much better than the shop ones.

BLACK CURRANT TEA

This is very good for colds, and as a preventative or relief for sore throats.

If the black currants are in season boil those and use the juice with some sugar added. But colds are not so prevalent when black currants are ripe; I expect if you have black currants in the garden you make jam from them, if not buy a good brand from the shop. A tablespoon of this jam in a glass of hot water is a quick way to make a soothing drink. To make it more nourishing for an invalid add the jam to a glass of hot milk.

117

COLTSFOOT TEA

This is very good for coughs; I can recommend this as we have often taken it.

Gather a few leaves of coltsfoot; they are big and thick, rather like an overgrown primrose leaf; so you will not need many. Put them in a saucepan with a pint of water and simmer for twenty minutes. Add the juice of a lemon and some strips of peel, and simmer for another five minutes. Strain the liquid off and sweeten to taste with honey or brown sugar. It can be kept for a few days, but as I said before it will turn into wine if kept too long.

CARAWAY SEED TEA

These can be grown in the garden, the plants look very much like carrots while growing. The seeds are good for flatulency, and from the taste of caraway seed tea I should imagine that gripe water for babies is made from the same thing. With a little sugar added the tea is quite a pleasant drink. I like it, but then I always did pinch the baby's gripe water.

Crush the seeds, or buy the already rolled ones; you will need half an ounce to half a pint of water. Put the seeds in a jug and pour on half a pint of boiling water, stir well then cover the jug and leave to stand overnight. I usually add some sugar when the mixture is hot. Strain the liquid off and bottle it, put the cork in tight. But don't keep it more than a week or so; it is best to make a small amount and have it fresh. A spoonful of this will relieve the "wind".

CARROT TEA

This is supposed to relieve gout. I don't suffer from

it, not yet anyway, so cannot vouch for the cure, but I have been told it is good.

Scrub a large carrot and slice it thinly into a saucepan, add half a pint of water, put the lid on and boil for forty minutes. Strain off the carrot liquid and drink a cup of this night and morning.

I expect the treatment would have to be continued for some time to have any effect.

CAMOMILE FLOWERS TEA

These are for clearing the blood and to relieve headaches. The dried flowers can be bought from the chemist.

Put a pinch of the flowers in a cup and pour on boiling water. Cover the cup and leave it for about five minutes, then drink it while still hot.

CELERY TEA

This is good for rheumatism they say, either the stalk or the seed can be used.

Boil a few stalks of celery or $\frac{1}{2}$ oz. of seed in a pint of water for about half an hour, then strain the liquid off and take a glass every day.

I believe eating raw celery is believed to be equally beneficial, but some people find this hard to digest.

CLOVE TEA

This is also good for flatulency.

Put four or five cloves in a small cup and pour on boiling water. Crush the cloves a little then cover the cup and leave for five minutes, sip it while it is hot.

HOP TEA

Hops seem to be a cure for numerous complaints, they act as a tonic, an aid to indigestion, to regain a lost appetite and many other things. No wonder beer is so popular. Taken hot hop tea is good for sleeplessness.

Put a handful of hops in a jug and pour on a pint of boiling water. Cover the jug and leave till cold. Take a small glass when necessary.

MARJORAM TEA

This is said to relieve headaches.

Put a teaspoon of marjoram leaves, fresh or dried in a teacup and pour on boiling water. Cover the cup with a saucer and leave for about five minutes then sip it while hot.

MINT TEA

This is also good for headaches and helps to relieve flatulence. I think it is quite pleasant to drink.

Put a few leaves, dried or fresh in a cup and pour on boiling water, cover the cup and leave for a few minutes. Sip it while hot. For flatulence add a pinch of bicarbonate of soda.

RASPBERRY LEAF TEA

This is also good as a gargle for sore throats and many people believe that it helps in making confinements easier if taken regularly beforehand. I do not know if doctors agree with this, but it is a very widely known remedy.

Pick a handful of raspberry leaves, or use dried ones. Put them in a jug and pour on half a pint of boiling water, stir well then cover the jug and leave for five minutes. Some people prefer to put the water and leaves in a saucepan and bring to the boil, they say that more of the goodness of the leaves is obtained this way. Always drink the tea hot, but cool it a little of course for a gargle.

ROSEMARY TEA

Here is yet another cure for headaches, it also makes a good hairwash.

Pick a few rosemary flowers and put them in a cup, pour on boiling water and cover the cup with a saucer and leave to infuse for five minutes. Sip slowly while hot. For a hairwash make larger quantities and use as a rinse.

SAGE TEA

This can be used as a gargle or as a hairwash; it is supposed to darken the hair and prevent greyness.

To make it you need a handful of fresh or dried sage leaves, put these in a jug and pour on a pint of boiling water, stir it well then cover the jug and leave it to get cold. Strain and use as a gargle or hairwash.

STRAWBERRY LEAF TEA

This is said to help diarrhoea.

Pick and wash a handful of strawberry leaves, and put them in a cup. Pour on boiling water and press well with a spoon, then cover the cup and leave for five minutes. Sip it while hot.

121

THYME TEA

This is very good to ease whooping cough, a little taken when the cough is troublesome is said to bring speedy relief. It can also be used as a gargle for sore throats.

Put a small teaspoonful of fresh or dried thyme leaves in a cup and pour on boiling water. Cover the cup and leave it for a few minutes to infuse then sip it while hot, or cool it for a gargle.

DANDELION COFFEE

This is not a herb tea, but as it is a drink I thought I would include it. I have been told that dandelion roots make very good coffee, very much like the real thing. It is quite simple to make, scrub the root then bake it in a slow oven till it is quite dry. Grate it very finely, then use in the same way as coffee. I always mean to try it, but when I think of it I never seem to have a fork handy to dig the root. If the price of coffee goes up any more I certainly shall try it.

INDEX